Dan Heisman

Everyone's Second Chess Book

Second Edition, Revised and Expanded

MONGOOSE
Press

BOSTON

Publisher: Mongoose Press
1005 Boylston Street, Suite 324
Newton Highlands, MA 02461
info@mongoosepress.com
www.MongoosePress.com

ISBN: 978-1-936277-84-1

Distributed to the trade by National Book Network
custserv@nbnbooks.com, 800-462-6420
For all other sales inquiries please contact the Publisher.

Layout: Stanislav Makarov
Editor: Jorge Amador
Cover Design and Illustrations: Alex Krivenda
Printed in the United States of America

Contents

Preface to the Second Edition

Everyone's Second Chess Book was the third book I wrote, after *Elements of Positional Evaluation* and *The Improving Annotator*. But it was my first book to strike a chord in a wide readership (*Elements* was more of a cult classic). In a sense, *Everyone's* was the precursor to my very successful "Novice Nook" column at Chess Café, which seven times won the award for "Best Instruction" from the Chess Journalists of America.

After the first printing quickly sold out, we fixed a few typos and came out with a second printing, which also sold out fairly quickly. At some point the rights to the book came into dispute, and no more printings were made. As a result, used copies of *Everyone's* sold for astronomical amounts on the Internet, sometimes going for as much as $200 a copy! For a while I was selling autographed copies for about one-tenth as much, but few bothered to look at my website www.danheisman.com and order the much less expensive autographed copies from me! ☺

One problem with the first two printings was that the pictures all involved scholastic players. This was not my idea, as the title *"Everyone's..."* was correct. Some potential readers browsing through the book looked at the pictures and got the wrong idea that the book was just meant for young juniors. However, readers soon realized that this was far from the case, as the intended reader was *anyone* looking for a "second" chess book. Most of the examples of erroneous play could have (and have!) been made by inexperienced players of any age. Moreover, the intended audience's age was not a factor when I was writing the book. For this new edition, we have completely changed the pictures to be more appropriate to the material.

The first edition of *Everyone's* was rather a thin book. This was intentional, but that left plenty of room to add new material in a second edition without making the book too weighty. So, besides adding material to the existing sections, I have added a number of new chapters dealing with more of those "What do I do next to get better?" issues that made the first edition so popular.

As with all new editions, we have corrected either outdated or incorrect information from the first edition and edited for greater clarity. In this respect, I want to thank game reviewer Troy Duncan, with especially big kudos to second-edition editor Jorge Amador.

So here's hoping you did not have to pay $200 for the copy you are reading...!

Dan Heisman
Wynnewood, Pennsylvania, August 2017

Introduction

*E*veryone's Second Chess Book: You Can't Play What You Don't See is my third chess book. I like to think that this one, like the others, is unique and helpful, and that it contributes to the world of chess knowledge.

Almost all beginners' chess books are written with one of two ideas in mind:

1. To teach the student how the pieces move, along with a few basic principles; or
2. To provide a series of basic tactics exercises (pins, forks, double attacks, etc.) to help the beginner learn to spot simple combinations, and then to help him or her progress to more complex winning exercises.

However, based upon my chess teaching experience with hundreds of beginners, both young and old, there is a definite gap between the time when you learn the rules and the point at which doing tactical problems is feasible. This gap consists of the time period when the beginner's brain learns to recognize more easily the possible moves that each piece can make in a position (by both the beginner's pieces and his opponents'), as well as to understand the value of the pieces and to figure out when each piece is safe. *Everyone's* is designed to fill the gap between "how to play" books and "beginning tactics" books – it's the missing link.

Not many of these beginners' books attempt to cover the mental process that a novice player goes through during this gap. *Everyone's* covers quite a bit of this process by discussing the general term *"board vision,"* which has to do with how the brain – through memory, visual input, and pattern recognition – grows to understand what is happening on a chessboard.

The problem with the usual approach in beginning tactics books is that most beginners lack the board vision to remember and use the knowledge gained from the exercises. They need some experience between the time they learn the basic moves until the time they are able to consistently solve simple tactical exercises. For example, after they learn the rules and the moves, most beginners need time and experience just to recognize when their pieces are safe and how to count whether they come out even, ahead, or behind after exchanges. Almost all beginners need to master this step before they can learn how to win a piece through a pin.

Just as GM Andrew Soltis wrote the *Catalog of Chess Mistakes* for adults, this book provides the many "what to avoids" for beginning chessplayers. In addition, *Everyone's* provides a series of improvement tips that will help all beginning students improve their game at a rapid rate. These tips will primarily involve the concept of board vision, as introduced above.

It is true that non-blind chessplayers rely primarily on their eyes to provide information as to what is happening on the board, and therefore one could argue that almost all chess capabilities could be lumped under a name such as "board vision." So to be more precise, we will (for the most part) eliminate from our consideration any chess-related subject that is not primarily vision-oriented: knowledge of openings and endgames, mental "databases" on how to play certain tactics and types of positions, positional evaluation capabilities, and other similar chess knowledge. Eliminating these factors still leaves a broad range of subjects – especially those related to beginners learning how to recognize what is happening on a chessboard.

A cousin of board vision is *visualization*. Whereas board vision deals with understanding the position on the board as it stands before you, visualization is the ability to keep track of the pieces as you imagine possible move sequences when you analyze.

Many years ago, GM Nikolai Krogius wrote a book called *Chess Psychology*. But unlike other books on chess psychology, he wrote not only about "psyching out" your opponent or "playing like a tiger," but also categorized areas of psychological mistakes related to visualization, such as:

- *The retained image* – when analyzing a position, you accidentally visualize leaving a piece where it was, instead of realizing it was moved during the intended combination.

- *The inert image* – in unbalanced (especially winning) positions, the inability to suddenly switch the focus to a dynamically new counterchance of the opponent.

- *The advance image* – the imagined threats by a player's opponent become so strong that the player loses all objectivity in trying to deal with the perceived (but not necessarily actual) threat.

I claim that all of the above are primarily characteristics of *advanced play* – an extension to the very basic problems of board vision, those that dominate after one first learns how to play the game. Watching beginners play, I have found conclusively that the reason newcomers leave pieces *en prise* (in take for free) or miss simple tactics, is *not* necessarily because of their lack of knowledge (of tactics, for example), but simply because they lack the necessary board vision to "see" which enemy pieces are attacking a square – or even that any tactic at all is possible.

It is important to note that teaching a tactic to a beginner before they develop the necessary board vision produces diminishing returns, because the knowledge to use the tactic is hampered by the inability to see that the pieces involved are set up for the tactic. Until I understood this, I found it frustrating to show beginners basic pins and forks, only to see them completely miss these same tactics immediately thereafter during their games. Once I understood what was happening, I began to concentrate on helping beginners to develop better board vision as quickly as possible. *After* the beginner gained the necessary board vision capabilities, *then* they picked up tactics much more readily, as they could "see" what was happening when it occurred in their games.

This book deals with a broad range of "board vision" problems, concentrating mainly on those that occur during the *beginner* and *intermediate* levels – I think Krogius and others have done a fine job explaining what happens on the advanced level. Therefore, besides *Everyone's Second Chess Book*, we could also have named this book, *Developing Board Vision*; *Beginning Chess Psychology*; *Chess Thinking Development*; or even *Beginners' Chess Mistakes*. No matter the name, we will be examining the problems and mistakes chessplayers run into during the early stages of their chess development.

We will also cover some other important bits of information about rules, etiquette, etc. that pertain to the early period of chess development. Any helpful topic is fair game, especially if it helps beginning players. The general idea of this book is therefore not only to cover how one continues to advance at chess after learning how to make the moves, but also to provide *as much practical advice as* we can, both for players at this level and for those who are instructing them. We only assume that the reader knows what is taught in the most basic beginners' books: how to move the pieces; the basic rules regarding checkmate and draws; and algebraic notation for following the moves.

Everyone's is primarily aimed at the following readership:

- Chess instructors
- Scholastic chess sponsors
- Interested parents
- Beginning chessplayers, teenage level and above
- Anyone interested in how beginners learn to play (better) chess

Close to Home

Everyone's covers the lower- to medium-level student, with USCF ratings below 1400 – and for the most part, below 1000. These are the vast majority of beginning players, and the ones who make the kind of serious mistakes we will try to teach you to avoid.

After the movie *Searching for Bobby Fischer* was released in the 1990s, the U.S. Chess Federation (USCF) reported that the number of junior memberships soared from about 5,000 in 1990 to over 40,000 by 1998. Correspondingly, the median rating of USCF players has dropped from about 1500 to about 1100 as more youthful, beginning players enter the wonderful world of tournament play.

If you are wondering just how familiar I, a battle-scarred master, am with this lower level of play, consider the following example:

Black

White
White to move

"Delen is setting himself up to be checkmated."

I was talking to one of my best students, James. James was 11 at the time and his rating was almost up to 1800. We were at the 1996 World Open here in Philadelphia. The player playing White was my son, Delen, one of the favorites in the always unpredictable Under 1000 section.

James smiled in disbelief because, unlike me, he hadn't seen Delen commit self-mate countless times. Delen is a smart kid and, at age 13, had been playing tournament chess for six years. But just the fact that Delen was still in the Under 1000 section is enough to tell you that he played just for fun, and was not all that interested in improving (note: with his friends leading the way, three years later Delen's rating peaked at 1800).

1.   ♖xa7

Delen plays the correct move, but I know from his previous pattern that his selection is a sign of trouble. One of my primary guidelines for my students is, *"When you are winning you should Think Defense First. You don't have to win more; you should mainly make sure you won't draw or even lose."*

1...   ♖d8!

Now I really started to worry. Even though Black was a much weaker player than my son, he was setting up a couple of traps that would surely win the game if Delen didn't stay alert.

2.   ♖e1?

Again, not really a bad move, but one indicative of the wrong frame of mind.

What *should* White be thinking? He is up the exchange and two pawns, so if he removes all of Black's threats he will probably win. Therefore, in practice the best move for a player like Delen would be 2.h3!, removing all back-rank threats. At least Delen did not fall for the superficial "good" pin with 2.♖d1? when 2...♘e2+ 3.♔f1 (Delen might even play 3.♔h1??? allowing 3...♖xd1 mate) 3...♖xd1+ 4.♔xe2 would still win, although not nearly as easily.

2...   ♘e2+!

Black really has nothing to lose by playing this trap. I had taught Delen to write his move down first before making it, put his pencil over the move, make a sanity check of the board, and then – only if this check passed – finally touch his piece. Some of this Delen did, but unfortunately his entire process took about 3 seconds! This short time even included the sanity check, which consisted only of seeing if the knight was really unguarded.

Black

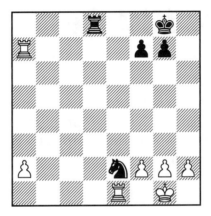

White
White to move

3. ♜xe2????   ♜d1 "mate"

Well, it was not really mate, but Delen's opponent said so and Delen resigned, as checkmate comes next move.

James looked at me, trying not to smile. Delen wasn't too upset, but as usual his master dad was trying to avoid apoplexy. If I die of a heart attack before you read this, now you will know why.

Chapter 1

//

Learning, Chunking, And Chess Mistakes

When humans learn a complex subject, such as reading or chess, they learn in "chunks" of information. These chunks gradually get more complex, the complexity corresponding to the level of information that the learner is currently able to process. For example, when a child learns reading, the levels representing these chunks are something like:

1. Recognizing which shapes are which letters
2. Remembering which letters make which sounds
3. Putting letters together to make multiple sounds, such as words
4. Recognizing words (and their meanings – although this is usually already known from learning how to talk)
5. Scanning several words, a line, or even multiple lines for content

There is a reading trick you may have seen. One puts the word "the" in a sentence twice consecutively, once at the end of a line and once at the start of the next. You then ask someone to read the sentence, which you place in the middle of a paragraph. Most experienced readers will not read both "the's". The reader's chunking capability at "reading level 5" makes this trick work.

When your reading chunks are at a higher level (adults with reading experience are almost all at level 5), then you can read quite a bit faster, but you no longer notice the individual words and letters in the same way you did when you were at a lower level. However, a beginning reader at level 3 or 4 will be processing one word at a time and, when presented with the double "the" trick, will usually see the two "the's."

Learning how to play chess can be thought of in exactly the same way. As you progress in chess experience, you will go through similar "levels":

1. Recognizing the pieces
2. Remembering how the pieces move
3. Determining legal moves for each piece
4. Determining reasonable moves for each piece
5. Seeing the whole board and determining reasonable plans for your entire set of pieces

I consider these chunking levels to be classified as "board vision" capabilities, because each is a cognitive problem the brain must deal with via the information obtained from visual input. Thus, a player looking at the board sees different things based upon his level, just as a non-football fan would not be able to recognize a blitzing linebacker when watching a game – instead, he might ask "what is a linebacker?"

The following provides an example of how a player at each level might think if he had Paul Morphy's position in this famous game:

Duke of Brunswick and Count Isouard

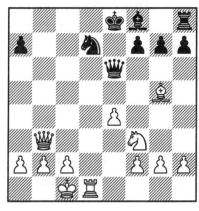

Morphy

Chapter 1

Level 1: *"Is that my queen or my king here close to me?"*

Level 2: *"Let's see, my knight moves like an 'L'."*

Level 3: *"Can that white rook jump over the black knight?"*

Level 4: *"If I move my queen up and check on b8, he can take me with his knight."*

Level 5: *"His back rank looks vulnerable to a mating attack. Can I clear the knight out of the way? Yes! After a queen check on b8, my rook can mate on d8."*

These attributes of board vision also explain why I could not play blindfold chess when I started, but could later; it is impossible to play blindfolded before you reach Level 5, but not so difficult for many Level 5 players (though of course they would differ greatly in blindfold ability, just as they do when they are looking at the board!).

An adult who is not a serious player but plays chess with his friends occasionally easily gets to Level 4 but may never get to Level 5, while a child playing tournament chess (very) seriously can reach Level 5 at a fairly young age, say eight or nine. The ability to play at Level 5 around age eight or nine for most youngsters would also explain, in part, why the USCF's Top 100 lists for each age group has the largest difference between the ratings of the "8 and Under" group versus the ratings of the "9-10" group (as opposed to, say, comparing the 17-18 group to the 15-16 group).

A note about USCF ratings: the higher the rating, the better. The top computers play around 3300; Magnus Carlsen, Garry Kasparov, and Bobby Fischer were all about 2800; master level starts at 2200; and no one can have a rating below 100.

Here are common board vision problems for lower-rated players:

- Under 100 (Level 1): Does not yet recognize all the pieces all the time.
- 100-200 (Level 2): Recognizes the pieces, but has trouble remembering how each piece moves.

- 200-400 (Level 3): Has trouble recognizing what the pieces can do, especially with regard to legality, such as moving into check or checking for illegal moves. During a game between two players at this level, board positions tend to be somewhat random. Players at this level often move very fast and "see" almost none of the possibilities; i.e., board vision tends to be almost non-existent.

- 400-600 (Low Level 4): Focuses almost exclusively on his own pieces; usually doesn't consider opponent's possibilities. Therefore puts pieces *en prise* constantly and still makes and allows illegal moves occasionally. Still tends to move very fast.

- 600-800 (Intermediate Level 4): Can chunk some of the board, but doesn't look for alternative moves; still has trouble taking into account the opponent's moves. Still puts pieces in take. Almost all of the game is legal. Tends to move relatively quickly without thinking of the consequences of their move or of the opponent's previous move.

- 800-1000 (Upper Level 4): Able to see the board but sometimes misses pieces on the perimeter (such as a faraway bishop); can make some plans but has no idea what is important in the position. Misses simple mates for both sides and still may put pieces in take occasionally. Still marked by Level 4 understanding; i.e., sees primarily parts of the board and piece moves, but doesn't chunk as much of the position as a Level 5 player would.

- 1000-1200 (Hazy area between Level 4 and Level 5): For the most part no longer puts pieces in take, but still has difficulty seeing and avoiding simple combinations. Has a tendency to come up with needlessly complex solutions to simple problems. Is able to see ahead on the board but still has difficulty understanding what is important in the position.

- 1200-1400: The beginning of higher-level chess. Players no longer just win because one just gave away more pieces than the other. Level 5 chunking is now becoming apparent in the player's analysis.

Chapter 1

Even adult players who are able to achieve Level 5 chunking may make enormous board vision errors when confronted with an unusual situation. At the 1970 Interzonal at Palma de Mallorca, during a tense endgame with both a pin and a pawn lever causing difficult tactics, a tired GM, Efim Geller, hallucinated against Bobby Fischer and made a famous mistake by thinking his king was pinning a pawn to a rook!

On a much more humorous level, two adults in the 1200-1500 range made the following unique board vision error at our local chess club:

Black

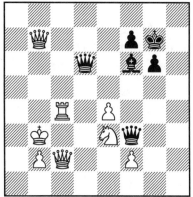

White

This unusual four-queen position was reached during a club game, and both players had less than five minutes left to complete the sudden-death time control. As the tournament director, I had retrieved two queens from another set for the second pair of queens (in other words, they were not playing with upside-down rooks). The second, borrowed "pair" were the queens on b7 and f3. The lack of board vision for unusual positions, even for relatively experienced adults, began to show as Black played the terrible 1...♛d3+???, putting his original queen *en prise* (attacked but not guarded). White hesitated longer than I would have, but played the obvious and correct 2.♕xd3.

Black

White
Position after 2.♕xd3

At this point *much* stranger things began to happen. White decided it might be a good idea if the player owning the borrowed two queens got those two pieces back. White therefore first picked up his capturing white queen, the original one *still on the board at d3*, and replaced the borrowed queen on b7 *but never putting back anything on d3(!!)*, and then took the captured black queen (the original one that was now *off* the board) and used it to replace the borrowed queen on f3, creating the following position (with only the set's original queens on the board) without any "chess" moves being made!!

Black

White
Position after returning the other set's queen(s)!

Yes, White has literally "Given away a queen" – the extra one with which he had made the capture on d3 is no longer on the board!! *Neither player noticed what had happened until I told them after the game!* How is it possible that experienced adult players could make such a mistake? I contend that it was because of the following factors:

- Both players were in time trouble and, under pressure, were not thinking clearly.

- The position was unusual, as both players had been playing with two queens. If the position had featured one queen each, then White would have certainly noticed if he (or anyone else) had given his only queen away. But since they were in a very rare position where he had two queens to one, it was much easier to "normalize" the position back to one queen each, as if the extra queens had been traded.

- The two extra queens had only been on the board for a few moves (which in real time, had only been a minute or two), so that it was easier for White to miss the fact that the position had changed drastically and he was now up a queen! I don't think this would have happened if the players had been rated closer to 2000.

Returning to chess development, there is another aspect that should be mentioned, and that is the issue of age and brain development. For example, almost all players below approximately age 8 have a difficult time "caring" about their opponent's moves. They have fun moving their pieces as a type of "problem solving," but no interest in the other player or solving problems that their opponent poses to them. This seems to be directly correlated with personal development away from chess, as the ego is strong, but the perception of others' feelings (empathy) is not yet well developed. As players get older and better, they begin to realize that it is equally as important (during one's move) to solve the problems the opponent is making for them as it is to pose those problems for that opponent. (Note: in chess, when one has the *initiative,* he is *posing* more of these problems, and when his opponent has the initiative the player is *solving* more of them.)

Most chess books are written either for absolute beginners (getting you quickly from Level 1 through Level 3) or for experienced players looking to get better (Low to high Level 5). Unfortunately, most chess-playing children are either at Level 4 or do not yet have the intellectual development to fully operate at Level 5. In addition, as was a central theme in my book, *Elements of Positional Evaluation,* many players are incorrectly taught stringent "rules" that should be learned as nothing more than helpful "guidelines," and thus continue to make the kind of mistakes we will discuss in later chapters.

Therefore, there is somewhat of a gap in the chess literature. We will try to address some of the most common kids' mistakes, especially at Level 4, through a series of examples, most from actual games from my students. For each example, we will try to examine why the mistake occurred and what general thinking guidelines would help you (or someone you are teaching) to avoid making a similar mistake.

The Eleven Most Common Mistakes
Of Players Rated 800-1400

800-1400 is the USCF rating of most of my students when they begin lessons. I see students in this range make the same mistakes over and over again. The following is a "Top-10 List" of the most common mistakes – almost all of them related to either board vision or inexperience:

1. Missing a simple tactic

Since being tactically sound is the main prerequisite for becoming an intermediate player, it follows that all beginners need to improve on their tactics. Not just combinations, but even simple motifs such as the most basic, counting (i.e., determining when a series of captures gains or loses material), as well as the standards such as pins, double attacks, x-rays, queening, forks, removal of the guard, overworked piece, interference, etc.

Note that it is far more common to miss (allow) a simple tactic by the opponent and lose material than it is to overlook an offensive tactic and fail to win material. That is because most weaker players are far more interested in what their own pieces can do, and also because most tactics books concentrate on how to win pieces, but not on how to avoid losing pieces. I address this latter problem in my book, *Is Your Move Safe?* (Mongoose Press, 2016).

The big tip here is to take time to ask the following about each of your candidate moves: *"If I make this move, does my opponent have in reply a check, a capture, or a threat that I cannot meet next move?"* If so, then that candidate move may have to be discarded. If this is the only thing you learn from this book, it may have been worth it...

2. Not determining all of the things the opponent can do (e.g., not considering all of the opponent's threats)

Beginners, especially youngsters, have a tendency to be "overwhelmed" (or preoccupied) with their own possibilities. Often the opponent makes a simple threat and a simple "What can he do to me now that he couldn't do to me before?" would suffice. Especially onerous seem to be discovered threats or threats from fast pieces (like bishops) from across the board. A suggestion: every time your opponent moves, ask yourself, *"What are ALL the things that move does?"*

3. Not getting all the pieces into play

Of all the problems on the list, this is the most perplexing. Often I have very bright, mature students, who simply cannot follow this guideline. I guess they are seduced by the forces of the "Dark Side." Some years ago John Keir, a parent of one of my students, was playing in his second tournament. He easily swept aside all six opponents in his Under 1200 section, taking home some nice first-place money. I immediately asked him how he did it. "Simple," John said, "All I did was pay attention when you were giving Clayton lessons about how important it was to get all your pieces in the game and I did. My opponents did not and I just got a good game and won!" If only I could bottle this attitude and sell it. Unfortunately most of my younger – and older! – students want to do something as soon as possible and don't have the patience to wait until all the forces are ready.

4. Not knowing basic opening traps

It is unfortunate, but playing good chess requires not just skill but also knowledge. Even beginners need to be schooled on some of the most basic opening traps in the openings they play. One player from our club, who has never taken any lessons or read any books but has a world of talent, lost in the opening after getting a bad position out of Black's side of the Fried Liver Attack, which he knew nothing about. Just a couple of hours of going over his basic opening moves would have allowed him to avoid Black's inferior fifth move in the sequence 1.e4 e5 2.♘f3 ♘c6 3.♗c4 ♘f6 4.♘g5 d5 5.exd5 ♘xd5?.

5. Phantom fears

While a common error, this one is not so easy to correct for the improving player. This problem entails a kind of "lazy thinking" whereby the beginner does not actually analyze to see if a continuation is possible, but rather assumes the opponent can or might do something harmful. Unfortunately, this type of analysis is often faulty, and the beginner often bypasses the correct continuation for fear of something that's totally impossible or easily preventable.

6. Excessive worry about the value of the pieces

I call this one of the "Reinfeld" problems (named after author Fred Reinfeld), and it is becoming more widely recognized. The problem is that assigning point values to the pieces is such a useful and necessary "principle" to beginners that they often don't get the follow-up: these values are not absolute, nor are the values given to beginners perfectly accurate! Play the position. For example, everyone understands that in the endgame it is better to have only one pawn left than to have one knight because knights can't mate, but a pawn can become a queen that does mate, but unfortunately novices are unable to carry over this concept in general – that material is relative and in some positions that fianchettoed bishop or outpost knight may be doing a lot more than a rook stuck behind closed lines.

7. Excessive worry about positional liabilities

I call this the "I don't want to win the queen because then my pawns are doubled" problem. Beginners need to understand that positional considerations are great tiebreaks when the material is even, but once one side goes up a piece or more, considerations like trading off your opponent's attacking material are almost always much more important than whether you might get doubled pawns in the process. As another example, *accepting doubled pawns is almost always a far less serious mistake than unnecessarily trading pieces* (but not necessarily pawns) *when you are losing*.

8. Playing too fast

It only took my son seven years of tournament play before he realized that he might actually see a little more and be a little more careful if he took his time. I always say, "The Powers That Be gave you the talent and the Tournament Director gave you the time, so use both to the maximum extent possible!" Board vision and the use of time go hand in hand, so the next chapter will deal with this interesting topic.

Sit on your hands!

Some tips for slowing down (see the next chapter for more detailed information):

- Sit on your hands so you don't move as soon as your opponent does.
- If you see a good move, don't play it. Look for a better one.
- Realize your brains are not in your fingers.
- Playing fast almost always helps your opponent.
- All the good players play at least somewhat slow, and there is good reason for this.

Note: less frequent, but not rare, is Playing Too Slow. Instead, you want to follow *The Goldilocks Principle* and pace yourself to use almost all your time without getting into unnecessary time pressure.

9. Not looking for a better move

As mentioned above, "If you see a good move, look for a better one!" Beginners are sometimes so overjoyed that their move looks good, that they don't realize sometimes there are much better moves available. In one of his early games, my son saw that he could take a pawn with check, so he did so in a split second. Unfortunately, the check lost by force, while instead he could have played mate in one if he had just looked for a few seconds.

10. Being afraid of the opponent

I often hear from players rated X, "Uh-oh, I am playing someone rated X+200. I am sure to lose." This is bad for several reasons:

- According to the rating system, even if the ratings were perfectly accurate, you will still win 24% of the points from someone 200 points higher rated.
- If you think you will lose, you probably will, especially since chess is a mental sport and thinking you will lose is a mental attitude.
- As a master, I have to admit it sounds a little silly when an 1100 player tells me how good a 1300 player is; after all, if 1300 is so good, how come the average experienced tourna-

ment player is rated well above that, and a 1300 rating is just about the bottom of the USCF's Top-100 list for 9-10 year olds! It is just a relative state of mind that a beginner has to overcome. I always say that *When you lose your fear of players with a certain rating, only then is it possible that you can become that rating.*

BONUS MISTAKE #11
11. Worrying about your rating

Ratings are fun and nice, but *your rating just follows your playing strength.* In the long run, your rating does not go up or down because of any particular set of wins and losses, but because you get better or, less hopefully, worse. If you want your rating to go up, don't worry about losing, worry about learning. And, paradoxically, if you are one of those who can learn by their mistakes and not repeat them (too much), then by losing you will learn more and, in the long run, get a higher rating. That is why I advise my students to play opponents, human and computer, that are about 200 rating points above them – just enough to push them and not enough to discourage them.

> If you want your rating to go up, don't worry about losing, worry about learning.

Losing

In some of the above discussion, we touched upon the fear of losing. An understanding of losing and how it affects a player is a subject worthy of an entire book. However, although this is not that book, losing has such a strong effect on beginners (and is so misunderstood by them) that our subtitle *You Can't Play What You Don't See* would not be complete unless we addressed the subject in at least some detail.

There is a spectrum of how a player is affected by losing, from "It doesn't bother me at all" to "I hate losing; I don't want to play because I might lose." Players at both ends of the spectrum don't advance very far in chess. Those who don't care at all about losing are usually doomed to repeat their mistakes over and over again, because they don't have any motivation to find out what they did wrong and to correct it. Those who are paralyzed by losing (it is too much of a blow to their ego) become paralyzed by the prospect of playing, and thus eventually stop. I will give the stories of three players to illustrate these concepts.

My son doesn't let much bother him, including losing. Therefore he was back-rank mated (as shown in the Introduction) about twenty times – many in otherwise winning positions – before he finally outgrew it. He just didn't feel it painful enough to lose in a winning position that he would do the work to check and make sure there was no mate. Of course, his father will live a few years less because of this.

Another one of my college-age friends got to the expert level, but hated to lose. One time he lost a game at our local club and sat on the window sill, beet red, for over an hour, refusing to answer any questions. Soon thereafter, he quit chess forever.

The third player's case was more curious. He was the brightest in his high-school class. However, there were many other fine chessplayers in his school, and they were all more experienced than he was. His friends, though, did not understand the great amount of time it takes to absorb the knowledge needed to improve. They said to him, *"How can you be the smartest kid in the school and not even be able to play higher than fifth board on the chess team?"* This drove him to distraction, and he couldn't bear the burden of not being the best right away. He, too, gave up the Royal Game.

All the best players of the game fall somewhere in between these two extremes, although sometimes slightly toward the "I hate to lose" side. They need to hate to lose just enough to be driven to learn what it takes to lose less often – no matter what the level of competition. But they cannot hate to lose so much that they will not study and learn from their losses.

Chapter 1

Objectively, one must look at losing not as a loss of ego, but as a learning experience. If every time you lose, you learn the cause of the loss and make a positive correction for the future, you will soon be a good player. It goes without saying that you usually learn more from losing than from winning. This is because losing always involves a mistake of a magnitude worth noting, and also because the opponents you lose to are, by definition, usually superior to the ones you beat, and thus are better able to demonstrate something worth learning.

It is worth repeating: you learn more when you lose, and getting better involves both acquiring more knowledge *and* developing your skills. Therefore those who play stronger players enough to lose often and are willing to learn from their losses (write down your games and go over them with your instructor!...) will get better the fastest. I always tell my beginning classes that I have undoubtedly lost more games than all of them put together...!

So next time your instructor is going over your game and tells you, *"that is a bad move,"* don't take it personally! He is trying to point out to you the kinds of mistakes you are making so that you will recognize them and, hopefully, not repeat the same mistakes whenever a similar situation arises.

Fear of losing can also cause students to ask for or agree to premature *draws*. What makes you a better player is more knowledge (your innate ability is always the same!). Many students feel that drawing, especially with a higher-rated player, will raise their rating. While this logic is obviously true, it is also rather shortsighted and superficial. What really raises your rating *in the long run* is becoming a better player – having a higher playing strength. More knowledge raises your playing strength and, in an accurate rating system like the USCF's, your rating will tend to move toward your playing strength. Therefore, losing a long endgame and learning something from it is eventually better for your rating than agreeing to a draw at the start of the endgame due to fear of losing! Realizing this truth is an important part of becoming a good player. *I tell my students to think of premature draw offers by their opponent as "offers to stay ignorant."* It is no coincidence that none of the world's best players got their high playing strength by drawing with a bunch of other players when they were learning, or that Bobby Fischer used to turn down draws almost without considering the position!

One of my students played a game where he agreed to a draw at the start of the endgame even though he was definitely not losing. When I asked him why he agreed to the draw, he said that he doesn't play the endgame very well, so he took the draw! I said, *"Hmmm, let me see. You don't play the endgame very well, so you avoid the endgame. Does that make any sense? How are you going to improve your endgame if you try to avoid it whenever possible?"*

> One of the best ways to improve is to analyze frequently with strong players.

It makes sense that if you want to improve, you should:

- Learn more about chess through professional instructors, books, videos, computers, etc.;
- Play as much as possible, both in the number of games *and in the number of moves;* and
- Get feedback on your games from your opponents, strong players/instructors, computer chess engines, and opening books/databases. Use every good resource at your disposal. You want to minimize your chances of repeatedly making the same mistakes.

Chapter 2

///

Developing Board Vision
And Visualization

2.1 Developing Visualization to Reinforce
Where the Pieces Can Move

There is no doubt: almost all good players initially developed their visualization – and board vision – by playing hundreds and thousands of chess games. But that doesn't mean that playing is the only way to develop visualization; it just means that most players were never exposed to any other method. In fact, even talented beginners are at first overwhelmed by the initial setup of the pieces and need quite a bit of playing time before they can readily "see" where all the pieces can move (of course we are discussing what happens *after* the rules for moving each piece have been explained to them). Partly for this reason, many chess teachers believe that starting with some simple endgame positions is easier for a beginner to comprehend.

It is possible to take this line of reasoning one step further and aid the development of visualization and board vision through a set of exercises which focus on one (or a few) pieces at a time. Steve Shutt, of the famous Masterman (Philadelphia) High School chess program, suggested some exercises to me and, using his ideas, I developed a few of my own. The following are some examples:

1. Pawn-taking

The student starts with one piece on any square (it is probably a good idea to do this exercise with each piece, in the order of increasing difficulty of piece movement: rook, then bishop, king, queen, and lastly, knight). The tutor then puts a pawn of the opposite color on the board (e.g., if the student has a white rook, then the tutor places black pawns). If the student can take it with the piece, he does so and quickly returns the captured pawn to the tutor; if he cannot capture the pawn, he just waits. The tutor continues to put pawns on the board one at a time. When multiple pawns are on the board and one is taken, the student may continue to take more pawns so long as he can do so with one additional piece move (in other words, if taking another pawn would require more than one additional move, he may *not* do so). The tutor should place some pawns where they can be taken and some where they cannot be taken. The exercise should continue until the student gets a "feel" for how the practice piece moves.

2. Pawn-taking with obstacles

In this variation, the student gets a specified number of consecutive moves to capture one pawn of the opposite color. The catch is that he may not move through or to certain squares where the tutor has placed pawns of the color of the student's piece. An example will illustrate this clearly: the tutor puts a black pawn on an empty board, along with a white rook which cannot capture the pawn in one move. There are always two ways the student can capture the pawn in two moves:

**The rook can capture the pawn
in two moves via f6 or b3**

After the student successfully captures the pawns via one of the two routes f6-b6 or b3-b6 – let's say, f6-b6 – then the tutor places a pawn somewhere on the f6-b6 path (e.g., on f5) so that the rook can no longer successfully use that path to capture the pawn in two moves.

**Now the rook can only capture the pawn
in two moves via b3**

Once the student has found the only remaining path to capture the pawn in two moves (b3-b6), a second white pawn is placed on the board on that path (e.g., on c3) so that now both two-move paths are blocked and it requires three moves to capture the pawn on b6.

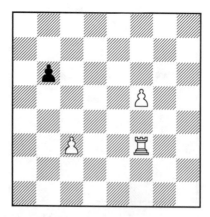

**Now the rook needs three moves to capture the pawn.
All legal first moves are possible.**

As the student continues to find paths to capture the pawn in three moves, these paths are also blocked by the tutor with a pawn:

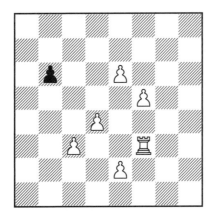

**In the final position, the rook can only
capture the pawn in three moves via f1**

This exercise continues with a piece until the student learns to successfully look for multiple ways that a piece can reach a destination. This exercise thus helps develop not only board vision, but also look-ahead and planning skills.

3. Ruler force fields

In this exercise the student puts a rook, bishop, or queen on the board. He then uses one or more rulers to show the lines of force "emanating" from the piece. For knights and kings, the student should put pawns on the board representing all the legal moves of the piece.

4. Knight "Tours"

There are many variations on this theme. The simplest one is to have the student put a knight on the board and have the tutor point to a square. The student then tries to move the knight to that square with the minimum number of moves (or as quickly as possible). In a second variation, the knight must find its way from one corner to another. These tasks can be made more difficult by placing pawns (obstacles) on the board which make the squares they are on inaccessible. For more advanced students, the task can be made harder still by extending this rule so that not only are the squares the pawns are on inaccessible, but so are the *squares the pawns attack!*

This latter exercise is exemplified by the "Chess IQ" test, which I first saw when it was published over forty years ago in *Chess Life*:

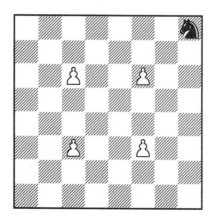

The "Chess IQ" Test

For this exercise, the student must find legal black knight moves to go, in order, from h8 to g8 to f8 to ... a8 to a7 to c7 to f7 to h7 to h6 ...zigzagging left, then right, and then back again until reaching all of the squares along the first rank (h1 is the final square). The student must avoid moving to any squares where the white pawns reside *as well as the ones they attack*. In other words, b7, d7, e7, g7, c6, f6, etc. can never be landed upon during the entire exercise – they are neither target squares nor can be used to get to target squares! The test is timed.

The original article on this test said that once a student has a modicum of board vision, this exercise can be used to test aptitude "independent" of chess knowledge. The student is supposed to take the test twice, one trial right after another. The tutor adds a penalty for each illegal move (I think the penalty was 10 seconds). The speed of the first test measures raw aptitude and the gain in time for the second try measures learning ability. Supposedly a first attempt taking five minutes or less shows international master potential, while three minutes or less shows grandmaster potential. (Believe it or not, the first time I took the test it took me about two minutes! And, after some practice, I was able to do it in less than a minute! – but since I started playing serious chess at 16, I knew I never was going to become a grandmaster, but that is another story – see my second book, *The Improving Annotator: From Beginner to Master*).

5. Dan's special knight obstacle course

This is a variation many students love – especially those who love mazes. I place a knight and a king of the opposite color on the board in any position except a knight's move apart. I then add many obstacles in the form of all the other pieces (it doesn't matter their color – only the knight and the opposing king matter). The knight has to make as many consecutive knight moves as it takes to "capture" the king. The following are some (increasingly harder) simple "Obstacle Courses" with the white knight trying to capture the black ling and the white pawns as obstacles:

A. This maze for beginners requires care to get to f2, such as: ♘b6-c4-b2-d1-f2-xh1

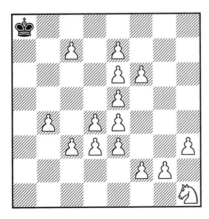

B. This easy maze has many solutions, such as ♘g3-f5-d6-c8-b6-xa8

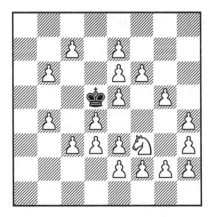

C. This slightly harder maze has also many solutions, such as ♘d2-e4-g3-h5-f4-xd5

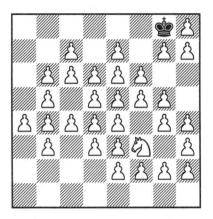

D. White must go something like ♘d2-f1-g3-h5-f4-g6-f8-d7-b8-a6-c5-b7-d8-f7-h6xg8!
(To make the above easier, remove the pawn on b4 or the one at h8!)

(see diagram next page)

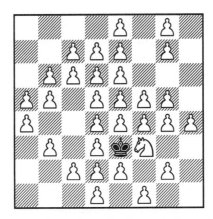

**E. Here, try ♘g1-h3-f2-h1-g3-h5-f6-h7-f8-
g6-h8-f7-d8-b7-c5-a6-b4-a2-c3-b1-a3-c4-xe3!**

The above exercises can be done with other pieces, such as rooks and bishops, although the knight is the most "fun."

2.2 Developing Checkmate (Tactical) Vision

There is a difference between recognizing (statically) what is a checkmate and learning how to give (dynamically) a simple (♕, ♕+♖, 2 ♕'s, 2 ♖'s, ♖) checkmate.

In fact, after teaching hundreds of elementary school children who initially didn't know how to move the pieces (as part of the inner city Chess in Schools' *Get Smart* program, I can state that understanding the concept of checkmate was much harder than, say, learning to name all the squares.

One of the problems is that checkmate is abstract – you never take off a king; you just have to prove that you could do it next move. It is somewhat like teaching children the difference between a *capture* and an *attack;* with a capture you take off a piece permanently, while with an attack you merely threaten to do so *next move.* Similarly, check is just an attack on a king, while checkmate indicates that the threat cannot be parried and that there is no legal move to get out of check. Then one has to explain that the rules do not allow some plausible defenses – such as counterattacking the opponent's king or even attacking *(but not capturing!)* the piece that is checking the king. In checkers, it is all much simpler – take off all the opponent's pieces and you win. In Monopoly, get everyone else's money. But, in chess, if your opponent moves his king into check, you not only cannot win by taking it off the board, you must "help" your opponent by telling him that the move is illegal and making him make a legal one. Many a game seems to have been won by my students who declared "I won. I took off his king..."

Therefore, Steve Shutt's suggestion to teach checkmate by example makes sense. Using an extension of the "Ruler Force Field" exercise, he uses the two-rook mate whereby the rooks force the king up the board (for initial checkmate definition, the king cannot approach the rooks!):

Defining mate by example:

"Force fields" emanate out of the left side of the rooks as the king is forced up the board:

1.♖h4+ ♔b5 2.♖g5+ ♔c6 3.♖h6+ ♔d7 4.♖g7+ ♔e8 5.♖h8 mate

One unfortunate drawback to this is that the concept of "definition" vs. "example" is not always clear in a fourth-grader's head. Even though I go to great pains to explain that checkmate is when an attacked king cannot get out of check, after showing this as an example I often get fed back the "definition": "Checkmate is when the rook is attacking the king and the king can't move..."! When I explain again that this was an example of checkmate but not my prior definition of checkmate, I still get second tries that start with, "Checkmate is when a rook..."

Once the concept of checkmate is established, there are two basic things that must be learned, in this order: 1) patterns of what is and isn't checkmate; and 2) how to force checkmate in the most common, simple cases (with just a ♕, ♕+♖, 2 ♕'s, 2 ♖'s, or just a ♖).

Visual aids can be used to illustrate multiple checkmate possibilities. For example, consider the position with only a white king on f2, a white queen on g4, and a black king on h1. The student is asked to find all the squares where the queen can successfully checkmate the black king. A white pawn can be placed on a square with a successful guess and a black pawn on a square for an unsuccessful guess (I sometimes put the pawns on the board lying sideways so that the student doesn't get confused and start to think there are actually pawns in the way!). After seven guesses (five successful), the board might look something like this:

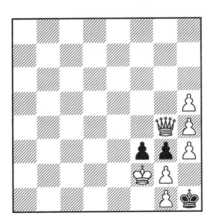

**Pawns indicate successful and
unsuccessful mate-in-1 guesses**

There are many ways to do these and many good books on the subject. László Polgár, father of the famous Polgár sisters, published a book of his problems which starts out with over 300 mate-in-one problems! Of course, doing these 300 helps establish how to recognize checkmate patterns and how to force it in one-move settings, but does not directly address what is *not* checkmate (except by the student's failed attempts...). Other books have problem sets of the type, "Which of the following positions is checkmate?", which directly focuses on this question. I think these types of problems are more beneficial *before* going the Polgár approach.

2.3 Developing the Ability to Count Material on Potential Exchanges

Tactical problems are designed to help the beginner learn to recognize combinations that either win material or give checkmate. However, as mentioned in the Introduction, a beginner is unable to do these tactical exercises until they recognize two more basic principles: 1) when a piece is being attacked and can be taken for free; and 2) evaluating potential exchanges to determine if they come out ahead, behind, or even (I call an exchange that comes out even "a fair trade"). The ability to calculate whether or not an exchange is favorable is necessary for the important ability to figure out whether a given piece is safe. This is especially true when the piece is on a square that is both attacked by some of the opponent's pieces and guarded by some of a player's other pieces.

Pieces that can be taken for free are said to be *"en prise."* I think the exercises earlier in this chapter about seeing where the pieces can go, as well as playing dozens of games, will help any beginner learn to recognize when either their or their opponent's pieces are *en prise.* The most important part of learning to recognize when pieces are *en prise* is learning to take your time and look around (see Chapter 6, "Board Vision and Time").

However, there are some exercises that can enhance a beginner's ability to see whether or not an exchange is favorable. I will give a few of these here, and any instructor or older beginner will be able to set up some more, once they see the idea. I call these "Counting" exercises. In the next chapter, we include a guideline on the values of the pieces: *As a rough guide (the Reinfeld values introduced in Chapter 1), consider knights and bishops as worth about 3 pawns, rooks 5 pawns, and queens 9. Pawns, of course, are worth 1.* We will use these values in the Counting exercises. Also, in these exercises we will *only* be considering the capture of the pawn on d3 even if other moves (or captures) are possible.

White to move: Is the black pawn safe?

The answer, of course, is "No." 1.♖xd3 would win the pawn. Too easy, you say? OK, let us build up the difficulty one step at a time. Since you have the pawn attacked once and it is guarded zero times, you can win it.

White to move: Is the black pawn safe?

Now the answer is "Yes;" after 1.♖xd3? ♖xd3, Black would be ahead by four pawns on that exchange (♖=5 minus ♙=1 equals 4 pawns ahead for Black). Therefore White, with the freedom to make any move he wanted, would almost undoubtedly not want to take the pawn. *We can see from this example that if a piece or pawn is guarded as many times as it is attacked, it is safe from capture as long as all the guarding pieces have the same value* (which, as we shall see shortly, is not always the case!).

White to move: Is the black pawn safe?

Now the answer is back to "No." After 1.♖(either)xd3 ♖xd3 2.♖xd3, White wins the pawn.

White to move: Is the black pawn safe?

The answer is "Yes." After 1.♖axd3? ♖xd3 2.♖xd3 ♖xd3, Black is again up four pawns.

White to move: Is the black pawn safe?

The answer is still "Yes." Substituting a queen for the black rook on the eighth rank makes no difference, because the queen can capture last: after 1.♖axd3? ♖xd3 2.♖xd3 ♕xd3 Black is again up four pawns.

White to move: Is the black pawn safe?

All of a sudden the problem isn't so trivial! With the queen in front of the black rook, any recapture must give up the queen: after 1.♖axd3 ♕xd3 2.♖xd3 ♖xd3, Black has captured two rooks (2 x 5 = 10), but had to give up a pawn and a queen (9 + 1 = 10), so the trade is actually approximately even. In this case, the pawn is still considered safe, but a valuable lesson is learned – *it matters in what order you can capture (or recapture) when determining whether a piece is safe.*

White to move: Is the black pawn safe?

This example shows that the *attacker's* order of capture also matters. The pawn is not safe as long as *White properly begins his capturing sequence with his lowest-value piece* – in this case, the knight: 1.♘xd3 wins the pawn. Notice that Black would be foolish to recapture, as 1.♘xd3 ♖xd3 2.♕xd3 wins the pawn and "the exchange" (defined as trading bishop or knight for a rook): White captures 5 + 1 = 6, while Black captures 3, so Black loses 3 instead of the 1 he would have lost if he had not recaptured. *Remember, you are never forced to recapture!* Chess is not checkers. Beginners almost always make the mistake of making all possible captures on a square once one has been initiated. If White had captured with the queen first, that would have been a huge mistake, as after 1.♕xd3? ♖xd3 2.♘xd3, White would lose the equivalent of 3 pawns – a queen (9) for a rook and pawn (5 + 1).

White to move: Is the black pawn on d3 safe?

All of White's pieces are ready to capture Black's pawn, but the d3-pawn is safe no matter how many times it is attacked, because the combined value of the attacked pawn on d3 plus its defender on c4 is always less than the value of any single capturing piece. So any capture on d3, such as 1.♘bxd3? cxd3 2.♘xd3, will cost White the equivalent of 3 pawns (a knight), while winning only two. (Yes, you can capture the pawn on c4, which is not guarded: 1.♘xc4, but that was not the question!)

One last example before I let you make up your own:

White to move: Is the black pawn safe?

This very important example shows that you just cannot count up the value of all the pieces that would be capturing on the square (except, of course, the final piece, which captures last and is not taken off the board). White should play 1.♗xd3, and if Black replies 1...♕xd3?, then White should play 2.♖xd3 ♖xd3 and then White should not recapture, but instead move his queen to safety, coming out about 2 pawns ahead (getting 9 + 1 and giving up 3 + 5). If instead White continued 3.♕xd3? ♖xd3, then White would have given up 3 + 5 + 9 = 17 and only gotten 1 + 9 + 5 = 15, losing two pawns' worth instead! Notice again that White not only does not *have to* capture 3.♕xd3 on the third move, but he *should* not. So the pawn is not safe. This example once again shows that *you should only do as much exchanging on a square as is favorable to you;*

any further exchanges that are not favorable are not forced and thus should be avoided.

> To determine if a capturing sequence is safe, you can't just count the number of attackers and defenders.

The above example should be sufficient to help the reader set up his own examples. The number of possible examples are immense (especially when the promotion of a pawn is involved!) and the more difficult ones can sometimes even cause an advanced player to pause. Set up some for yourself and practice until you think you have mastered the "safety" problem!

2.4 Developing Tactical Board Vision Based Upon Rating

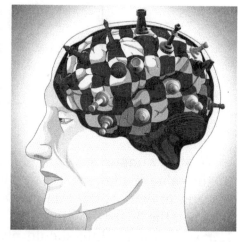

In a sense, *any* book on tactics is trying to help the student to develop tactical "vision." But we can separate tactical knowledge into two (admittedly not independent) parts: 1) those patterns which you have to recognize *may* contain a tactical element; and 2) the knowledge of tactical motifs and how to analyze them to see if there is a satisfactory "combination." We can also distinguish between beginners' exercises such as recognizing tactical motifs like a pin or fork and advanced topics such as the necessary preconditions for the classical bishop sacrifice (now often referred to as the "Greek Gift"). While the latter clearly falls under the topic of "Advanced Board Vision," this section will only deal with developing a novice's visual sense of legal moves and beginning tactical motifs.

What we need to do next is to repeat the level of board-vision understanding shown in the previous chapter and then develop a corresponding *plan for improvement* based upon that level:

1.   Rating Under 100 (Level 1): *Does not yet recognize all the pieces all the time.*

Plan: Players rated under 800 are usually young juniors. They need to play as much as possible. Players under the 100 level have just learned what the pieces are and may still have difficulty recognizing each correctly. These are usually very young players who just need to be reassured about all the piece names (relating the names to their medieval counterparts is usually interesting).

2.   100-200 (Level 2): *Recognizes the pieces, but has trouble remembering how each piece moves.*

Plan: For players just learning how each piece moves, sometimes it is better not to play with all the pieces at once. For example, just put a rook on the board and ask the player to name it and to show all the places where it can move in one turn. For youngsters, you have to get across the concept that each piece can only make one move at a time, just as each player takes a turn in Candyland or Checkers. For knight moves, I often have youngsters stand on a floor with squares and do a "Knight Dance," where each movement is a step two (or one) square in a direction followed by a step one (or two) squares in a direction orthogonal (at right angles) to the first step. We continue the "dance" until we have tried most of the possibilities several times (like one up and two right; two left and one down; two back and one left, etc.)

3.   200-400 (Level 3): *Has trouble recognizing what the pieces can do, especially with regard to legality, such as moving into check or checking for illegal moves. During a game between two players at this level the board positions tend to be somewhat random. Players at this level often move very fast and "see" almost none of the possibilities; i.e., board vision tends to be almost non-existent.*

Plan: For players at this level, again playing games with a subset of the pieces is a good start. Players at this level often have confusion between checkmate (which involves the concept that you prove you can take the king *next* move) and actually taking the king, which is illegal. In other words, they sometimes want to win the game when their opponent moves into check by taking the king. The concept that you not only don't win, but have to "help" your opponent by telling him that his/her move was illegal, is not trivial. Steve Shutt, the coach at Masterman, suggests that checkmate is best learned by example and suggests a two-rooks-vs.-king endgame. I usually perform that one with two rulers representing the "force fields" that prevent the king from escaping the mating net.

4. 400-600 (Low Level 4): *Focuses almost exclusively on his own pieces; usually doesn't consider opponent's possibilities. Therefore puts pieces in take ("en prise") constantly and still makes and allows illegal moves occasionally. Still tends to move very fast.*

Plan: This is the level most people see in youngsters (especially ages 6-8) who say "they can play chess." Because of the way that the brain develops, many children younger than age eight seem to have difficulty understanding that there are two players in every game and that each one is equally important! They focus exclusively on their own moves and rarely look at their opponent's moves. It is at this level that you should start making players aware of their opponent's pieces' possibilities by suggesting they ask, *"Are my pieces safe?"* and, *"Are there any of my opponent's pieces that are not safe?"* Similar questions would be, *"If I would move my piece there, can my opponent just take it off for free?"* or, *"Why did my opponent make that move?"*

At this level, keeping the pieces safe is the primary tactic, and the player who removes all of his opponent's pieces first either stumbles into a checkmate or draws by stalemating the opponent when the opponent is down to just a king. So it is good to introduce the concept of stalemate and tell the player who is winning overwhelmingly that the only way he won't win is by failing to figure out *before he touches a piece* whether his/her planned move allows his/her opponent a move. Getting these players to slow down is also a major challenge. Players at this level should be introduced to the dangers of the Scholar's Mate (e.g., 1.e4 e5 2.♕h5?! ♘c6 3.♗c4 ♘f6?? 4.♕xf7 mate), both in learning to defend against it as well as the drawbacks of trying to win with it!

5. 600-800: (Intermediate Level 4): *Can chunk some of the board, but doesn't look for alternative moves; still has trouble taking into*

account the opponent's moves. Still puts pieces in take. Almost all of the game is legal. Tends to move relatively quickly without thinking of the consequences of their move or opponent's previous move.

Plan: This is a common level for bright students 8-10 years old that have played at least a few dozen games with their family and friends. Being able to understand the concept of counting and almost perfectly execute the concept of safety is necessary for players at this level in order for them to progress to learning more advanced tactics. In other words, in order to progress toward the 800 level students not only should be able to answer the question, "Is that square adequately defended?," but also to think about piece safety for both players *on every move.* Once they can do so, they are ready to learn the basic tactical motifs from a textbook such as John Bain's *Chess Tactics for Students,* which deals with pins, forks, double attacks, removal of the guard, basic back-rank mates, skewers, pawn promotion, and so on. Students at the 800 level know at least some of these concepts fairly well, even if they cannot execute them consistently.

As for openings, the players at this level need to know that the three main things you are trying to do in the opening are:

- To develop *all* your pieces (and enough pawns to control space);
- To get some control of the center; and
- To castle your king into safety.

At this level they should also be able to mate with a queen and king vs. king and with two rooks and king vs. king fairly consistently, without stalemating or losing material.

6.   800-1000 (Upper Level 4): *Able to see the board, but sometimes misses pieces on the perimeter (such as a faraway bishop); can make some plans but has no idea what is important in the position. Misses simple mates for both sides and still may put pieces in take occasionally. Still marked by Level 4 understanding, i.e. sees primarily parts of the board and piece moves, but doesn't chunk as much of the position as a Level 5 player would.*

Plan: Many beginning adults start at this level. At this ability the player should be working through all the basic tactical motifs and should then be able to recognize them in game (and not just problem) conditions. The next step is to start to "combine" motifs, thus being able to pull off basic "combinations." For students with USCF ratings nearing 1000, I like to recommend continuing to use Bain's book, and other similar tactics books with basic patterns (my *Back to Basics: Tactics* book is one level more difficult than Bain's book). Since "chess is 99% tactics" (Teichmann), progressing through Bain and similar fundamental tactics books is the best way to improve their game (from the theory standpoint; of course, from the practice standpoint the best way, as always, is to play as many games as possible against players rated about 200 points above you). One of my students, age about 11, improved his rating from about 900 to about 1900 in approximately 18 months by taking lessons every week, going through tactics books, and playing incessantly on the Internet Chess Club (www.chessclub.com). Players at this level should be able to mate with a king and rook vs. king well within the 50-move draw rule limit (where if both sides make 50 consecutive moves without a piece being captured or a pawn moved, either side may claim a draw).

7.   1000-1200 (Hazy area between Level 4 and Level 5): *For the most part no longer puts pieces in take, but still has difficulty seeing and avoiding simple combinations. Has a tendency to come up with unnecessarily complex solutions to simple problems. Is able to see ahead on the board but still has difficulty understanding what is important in the position.*

Plan: At this level, all the players now know they have to pay attention to what their opponent is doing on every move. Their tactics are rudimentary, but they can hang on and play long games even against fairly good adults. They can recognize (not just solve) a decent percentage of the problems in Bain's book. Intelligent high-school players who play constantly are usually at least at this level. Strangely enough, players at this level seem to have trouble following the simple guideline, "Move every piece once before you move any piece twice, unless it wins material or prevents losing material." They often think that they are "too good" to follow this advice, and 95% of the time they are wrong. With one player this problem has become chronic, so I make him repeat the above guideline seven times every time he shows me a game where he consistently refuses to develop all his pieces. Of course, he has begun "losing" the scoresheet of those games where he knows I will make him do this!... Players at this level have almost always picked up their higher-rated brethren's concern for openings, and usually know some opening theory, although often they spend too much time learning opening theory. However, to be fair, a good chess coach should at least familiarize players at this level with any traps they can fall into with their opening repertoire, so that at least they do not often lose to better players right in the opening.

8.   1200-1400: *The beginning of higher-level chess. Players no longer win just because one side gave away more pieces than the other. Level 5 chunking is now becoming apparent in a player's analysis.*

Plan: Players at this level play "real chess" and often can give good games to players up to the expert level. I have a theory that for 99+% of games between two players rated under 1400, there will be at least one point during the game where one of the players makes a tactical mistake large enough to lose the game immediately. Of course, the opponent may not always take advantage of the mistake, so it may not decide the game! Therefore, a continued emphasis on tactics, especially checking to see if their own moves are safe, is still a dominant theme. Players at this level usually are quite familiar with their opening with White, and also know pretty well at least one defense to 1.d4 and 1.e4. They are also capable of winning many advantageous endgames where they are only up one pawn.

2.5 Be Imaginative

There is obviously a close correlation between board vision and imagination. But your imagination is not restricted to imagining board positions. Take the following example, which involves understanding how to count how many times a square is attacked:

The "Glory" Attack

When I am teaching "counting" to the lower-rated players, I want them to "see" multiple attacks like the above. However, after asking dozens of students how many times the knight on h8 is attacked, I was surprised at how many answered "one." I began to think about their answer, and decided it wasn't totally wrong. So I discussed this with one of my bright seven-year-old students and we decided to give the attacker behind the initial attacker a special name. He decided to name the secondary attackers after his dog, "Glory." Now this may sound silly, but now when I teach students about this type of attack and tell the story about Glory, they all remember!...

The above story may sound relatively unimportant, but any gimmick that makes learning fun and interesting is not unimportant. It is no coincidence that students quickly learn "Knight on the rim, your future is dim," but not so easily other similar concepts.

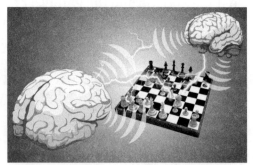

Board vision: imagination

And every student is different. Some learn well by going over games, and a few do not. Some like to go over problems, and for others this is drudgery. A good teacher should find out what media the student enjoys and gets the most benefits from: books, DVDs, flash cards, online videos, databases, etc. and try to gear the learning to the student. Obviously a visual student will learn better from a book, while one who is more comfortable with audio learning might benefit more from a DVD or online video. And students who are afraid that someone will make fun of them when they lose may have more fun playing against a computer, at least for a while. But remember:

If your goal is to be a good player against humans, you should practice primarily against humans.

Chapter 3

///

Board Vision and Beginners' Guidelines

The U.S. Chess Federation's *Official Chess Rulebook* has over 300 pages! But that one book on chess *rules* hardly compares with the many books devoted to chess *guidelines:* tips or maxims that help you play better and decide what move is best. This chapter will list quite a few guidelines for beginners – many are designed to enhance board vision in one way or another – and discuss them in the context of learning chess.

A guideline is called a "guideline" and not a rule usually because it is more general and has many possible exceptions. Despite the less stringent nature of a guideline, in my experience teaching players, I have found that one of their problems is that they know a principle but they find some clever (but wrong) way of not following it. So a "meta-principle" that is very helpful until you are a strong player is: *"If you know a principle and there are no tactics* (forcing sequences for either side which win material or checkmate) *or countering principles that would strongly hint that that principle does not apply here, then just follow that principle."* If more of my students followed this meta-principle instead of trying to be "clever," they would be stronger players.

> A Guideline/Principle differs from a Rule because it usually has many exceptions, and is meant as an aid, not something that must be followed.

Here is an example. Take the principle, "If a piece is attacked by a piece of a lesser value, the simplest thing to do is to just move the attacked piece." Suppose the game opens **1.e4 e6 2.d4 d5 3.♗d3?! ♘f6** (3...dxe4 followed by 4...♘f6 is more accurate) **4.e5:**

Black

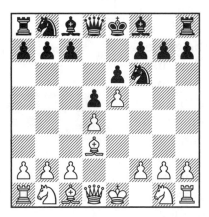

White
Black to move after 4.e5

According to the *AWL* (Attack it with something Worth Less) idea, Black should of course now move his knight to safety, e.g. 4...♘fd7. But many beginners think...

"He can't push me around! I will show him I don't have to move the knight!"

...and so they play **4...♗b4+??.** This sequence backfires when White simply plays **5.c3,** and now the knight at f6 and the bishop on b4 are both attacked and one of them will be lost. By not following the principle with a simple knight-saving move, Black has outsmarted himself and lost a piece. I see this type of mistake all the time!

With that in mind, here is our list of some helpful principles to keep in mind when you are playing:

1. Think and take your time.

This is the granddaddy of all chess maxims. Your goal is to use almost all the time on your clock every game without getting into unnecessary time pressure. When I am teaching I call this "Guideline Zero," because all the other guidelines are useless if you don't follow this one! One of my young students, who had been taking lessons for months, recently played in his second tournament. He finished all his games before all the other students did, and only managed to win one out of four. After the games, I asked him if he had used all the maxims I had taught him. He said no. I told him that *all the lessons in the world wouldn't help him play better chess if he didn't*

Hand hovering-itis

take the time to think about what he had learned... Chapter 6 is devoted entirely to the subject of helping students play slower. (By the way, my "Minus One" Guideline is "Have Fun").

2. Think with your head, not with your hands.

Keep your hands away from the table! You have nothing to win and everything to lose by touching pieces too fast. Remember, serious chess is played with the touch-move rules (if you purposely touch a piece, you have to move it; if you let go of a piece, you have to leave it there; if you intentionally touch an opponent's piece, you have to take it) – so there is nothing to be gained by touching a piece before you are *sure* you want to move it.

3. Before you move, visualize your possible moves and make sure *all* your pieces would be safe; conversely, look at your opponent's position – if one or more of his/her pieces are not safe, you might strongly consider taking them!

The best way to learn to do that – in addition to consciously taking your time and looking around the board – is to play hundreds of games, preferably with opponents (computers or humans) strong enough to take off your pieces when you leave them *en prise* (in take)! Almost all good players learned this way, and after a while you develop the visualization and board vision necessary to allow yourself to be careful!

4. If you see a good move, look for a better one!

All my students know this one, but only a few actually do it consistently when they learn it! You are always striving to play the *best* move in any position, and so if you find a better one, don't play that one either – look for an even better one. It is pretty simple logic that you can't prove what the best move is unless you have considered all of the reasonable ones! As a helpful hint, you should always look at all your *checks, captures, and threats* (and make sure to check to see your opponent's checks, captures, and threats, also!). Note that with the clock running you can't always find the best move, so we could extend your *goal on each move* to be: *Find the best move you can in a reasonable amount of time.*

5. You can't play what you don't see.

Until you develop the board vision or the patience to look for all possible moves and replies, it is impossible to evaluate properly. Without considering all the moves, it is impossible to decide which one is best. Beginners often cannot play the best move because they don't take the time to look all around the board and see the consequences of what they might do. And if you don't develop your visualization skills to "see" future possible positions clearly, then you won't be able to analyze and evaluate them properly.

6. In the opening, you have 3 main goals/objectives:

- **Activate *all* of your pieces** (but not all of your pawns) – A guideline to this effect is very important and thus worth emphasizing: *Try to move every piece (not pawn) once before you move any piece twice (unless there is a tactic).* While this is not always possible (especially when obeying guideline 3, keeping all your pieces safe), it is an important goal. Next to Counting (the ability to count captures on a square to calculate safety), this is *the most important opening concern* that I would emphasize to beginners – as well as some non-beginners. Consider castling a king move so that the castled rook still may need to be relocated to a better position.

59

- **Get some control of the center** – Usually by moving a center pawn or two up two spaces and moving your knights toward the center. Position your bishops so that they have some control over central squares.

- **Castle your king into safety** – Beginners, and some intermediates, who fail to do this either eventually learn to do so or are consistently beaten by those who do. I am often asked by beginners, "Why is castling so important?" Here are some answers:

    ○ Castling is the only move which helps put two pieces at once toward where they should be – so it *gains* a tempo, not loses one.

    ○ The king is initially safer toward a corner – the 90 degrees of attack are easier to defend than the 180 degrees in the center.

    ○ Importantly, not only can the castled rook now get to the center across the rank, but it also communicates and coordinates well with the queen and especially with the other rook.

7. In the opening, a general order of classical development might be:

"Knights Toward the Center
Then Bishops May Enter
Castle Your King...
Queen up a Little
Rooks to the Middle."

As a rough guide, move three to five pawns, and these should be pawns to either help control the center and/or get your bishops in the game. Rooks move to the middle – or to open and semi-open files – along the first rank, only rarely by moving the rook's pawns up and then moving the rooks up and over. Also, the knight and bishop on the side where the king will castle often move first, then castling, followed by the development of the other knight and bishop. Keep in mind the idea, *"He who uses his rooks best usually wins the opening."*

8. After the opening, when looking for your own or your opponent's best move(s), first try looking at (in order):

- **Checks,**
- **Captures,** and
- **Threats** – which are usually checks or captures you can do *next* move

These are called the "forcing moves." This guideline is also the key to finding the most important "candidate" moves in a position (moves that you should consider before deciding on a move). It is also a key to solving most tactical problems. But don't forget to consider *your opponent's* checks, captures, and threats as well as yours – especially as his response to your potential (candidate) moves.

9. As a *rough* guide, consider the average value of knights and bishops as about 3 pawns, rooks 5 pawns, and queens 9. Pawns, of course, are worth 1 (on average)!

The key word in this guideline is "about." The value of pieces changes depending upon the position, and even on the average the above values are only rough. When players get to an advanced level, they realize that relying too heavily on these beginner values can be dangerous. For example, a rook is worth a little less than 5 in many early-game positions, and a bishop or knight plus two pawns is usually worth more than a rook. Similarly, a bishop plus knight is usually worth more than a rook plus a pawn. Unfortunately, some very experienced players never seem to learn this lesson and, as a result, their development into an advanced player is definitely hampered.

Note that I express these values in terms of "pawns," not "points." Pawns exist and can be compared; points are abstract. I often address students on the value of the pieces and, after I tell them that no piece is always worth exactly N (pawns), sometimes they will ask me how many "points" a pawn is worth! So, if you think in terms of pawns and not points, you will not only avoid that pitfall, but also enhance the understanding that you are considering the relative value of material, and not some abstract "points."

As you get to be a better player, you will want the "advanced" averages: ♛=10 pawns; ♜=5.25; ♝=3.5; ♞=3.5. Using these values, "the exchange" (= winning a rook for a bishop or knight) is worth about 1¼ pawns. These numbers are courtesy of computer chess expert GM Larry Kaufman, who published these values in his advanced opening book *The Kaufman Repertoire in Black and White*.

> ### *Chart of Values* (advanced)
> Pawn..............1.00
> **Knight...........3.50**
> **Bishop...........3.50**
> **Rook..............5.25**
> **Queen...........10.00**
> **from Larry Kaufman's *Chess Life* Table**

10. Look at what your opponent is doing – your pieces are *not* more important than his!

After your opponent moves, ask yourself not just, *"Why did he make that move?"* but, even better:

"What are all *the things my opponent's move does?"* – if you miss even one, that could easily cost you the game!

Even very weak opponents have *some* reason for making a move – though it may not be a good reason. An associated question would be:

"What are all the things he can he do to me now that he couldn't do to me before?"

After all, if you properly figure this out each move, then the only new things you need to worry about were generated by your opponent's (or your) last move. Of course, if you miscalculated what he could do on the previous move, that miscalculation might still exist! Finally, be very aware that the new possibilities for your opponent are not just those of the piece he moved, but also any other piece that had a line opened up by that move or that was affected in any way. Many errors occur when beginners look at the opponent's moved piece, but not those newly opened lines. Consider the following position:

Black

White
Position after White plays e2-e4

White has just made the pawn move e2-e4. I give this artificial position to beginners and ask...

Show me all the new moves that White could make next move *that he couldn't before he played e2-e4* (Black is looking for "threats" – in the form of new possibilities for White created by the move e2-e4 – to help Black decide what he should do on his turn).

The correct answer is that there are 14 new moves for White that are now possible: ♗e2, ♗d3, ♗c4, ♗b5, ♗xa6, ♕e2, ♕f3, ♕g4, ♕xh5, ♔e2, ♘e2, exd5, exf5, and e4-e5 mate! Note that 11 of the 14 moves are by other pieces (via *discoveries),* the result of open lines created by moving the e-pawn, and not just future moves of the e-pawn.

It is not a coincidence that the one "straightforward" move that is made possible by moving the pawn to e4 – pawn to e5 – is designed to be mate! But it is also important that two of the diagonal moves are captures of the black knights "on the rim." Most beginners will usually not get this apparently simple problem correct without some prompting. This position is therefore a good illustration of the importance and power of asking yourself the question, *"What are* all *the things he can do to me now that he couldn't do to me before?"*

11. "Knight on the rim, your future is dim": Keep your pieces pointed toward the center.

Pieces lose mobility (some of their potential moves) when they are toward the edge – especially knights. In addition, the player who controls the center usually has the advantage; his pieces can get across the board much easier. Knights, being slower than bishops, rooks, and queens, are especially weakened when "out of the action" and are also more likely to get trapped. This guideline is also known as "knight on the rim – your future is grim."

12. When ahead pieces, trade pieces (but not necessarily pawns); when behind pieces, trade pawns.

When you have the advantage, trading off pieces leaves you with a bigger percentage lead and reduces enemy possibilities. A lone bishop or knight with a few pawns on each side is usually a trivial win, as the piece can coordinate with the king to double-attack pawns which the opponent cannot defend, usually leading to extra pawns that become queens. On the other hand, when you are down a bishop or knight, trading pawns makes the win harder, especially if there is the possibility of trading off all the pawns. This loss of all your pawns makes a win impossible, as a lone bishop or knight (along with the king) is not sufficient material to checkmate an opposing king.

13. The more you are winning, the more you should think "defense first;" the more you are losing, the more you should think offense. When winning easily, you should concentrate on stopping things the opponent can do to get back into the game.

This is a fairly complex guideline and is discussed in more detail in the next chapter, *"Don't Make Lemonade When You Should Be Making Ice Tea."*

In situations where one side has a large material advantage, it is silly to think that you must spend all your energy trying to get more material. A football team ahead 70-0 does not need to think about how to score more touchdowns.

Similarly, it makes sense that the side that is winning wants to keep things simple, while the side that is losing wants the position to be complicated. After all, a losing player literally has "nothing to lose" and wants to make it complicated so that the winning player has more chances to go wrong. If these complications just hasten the losing player's defeat, then at least he tried to get back in the game (you wouldn't take unnecessary chances when behind against a much weaker player, though, because prolonging the game against a much weaker player gives him more chances to go wrong...).

I have often seen beginners who were ahead a queen (i.e., had a queen more than their opponent) end up losing because they figured they would just use their queen to go around picking up pawns and, while they did this, their opponent either trapped their queen or got so far ahead in development that the opponent generated a mating attack.

> A football team ahead 70-0 does not need
> to think about how to score more touchdowns.

So when you are winning easily, the following important list contains practical guidelines to help you preserve your advantage:

- **Make sure you prevent easy patterns where you can be checkmated.**
  For example, provide your king with *Luft*, a space to move into in case he is checked on the back rank. If your opponent only has one bishop, the *Luft* square is often best on the opposite color of that bishop.

- **Get *all* your pieces out.**
  This guideline is even more important here than it is normally, when it is very important! When you are winning with more material, then bringing all this material to bear on your opponent's position is often more than he can defend. Also, if you bring all your pieces into play, it is much less likely that you will be mated, find yourself short of defense, or find yourself in a bad position because you are so far behind in development.

- **Keep It Simple (KIS).**
  You don't need complications to win – you've already won. So avoid crazy sacrifices, or complicated variations. Simple chess almost always wins when you are way ahead.

- **Pay attention to what your opponent is doing.**
  When you are winning, you have a lot to lose, so if you can parry all your opponent's current and future threats, he has a lot less chance of getting back in the game.

- **Make fair trades of pieces** (but not necessarily pawns). This both accentuates the advantage and removes your opponent's ability to attack and get back into the game. The corollary, *"When behind in material, avoid trades of pieces unless absolutely forced to,"* is one of the most important guidelines to follow if you want to fight back in bad positions.

14. If you can keep the game close, then, if you outplay your opponent during the crucial tactical portion(s) of the game, you will almost undoubtedly win.

While with most beginners, the motto *"Whoever makes the next to the last mistake wins"* often holds true as it does for more experienced players, I have found that telling my students to pay special attention – take your time! – when things get complicated is good advice. And slow players should make sure they have left enough time on the clock so that they are able to pay this attention when the situation arises.

15. Don't be too quick to "graduate" from basic tactics puzzles to intermediate.

Think of this like mathematics. You spend a great deal of time learning (memorizing) the multiplication tables so you just know that $6 \times 7 = 42$. But you don't spend the same amount of time learning how to do $456 \times 73,417$. Instead, once you learn the multiplication tables, you learn how to multiply multi-digit numbers and that suffices. Similarly, in chess there are possibly 2,000 basic and common patterns that not only occur repeatedly, but that form the basis for most intermediate and advanced tactical combinations. So it makes sense to learn as many of those 2,000 upside down and inside out before skipping ahead to doing only more advanced tactics.

16. Always play with confidence, aggression, and respect for your opponent's moves and ideas.

Too many players play with fear of their opponent, play passively against stronger opponents, and/or play with overconfidence and unnecessary speed versus weaker opponents. None of this is helpful. Chess is a mental game, so your mental state has much to do with how well you play. Any thoughts that are *not* directed toward the goal of *"What's the best move I can make in this position in a reasonable amount of time?"* are likely detrimental.

Many guidelines apply to particular positions – certain types of endgames, attacks, or maneuvers. Just a few are:

- **Don't move out your queen early where it can just be easily attacked by other pieces as they naturally develop.**
  Importantly, you can expand this principle to any piece that can be attacked by pieces of a lesser value. So the more general principle is: *Don't place pieces where your opponent's pieces of lesser value can easily attack them while moving onto favorable squares.* I call this idea *"AWL"* (Attack with something Worth Less).

- **Passed pawns must be pushed** (but not past their zone of protection).
  The closer they are to promoting, the more dangerous they become.

- **Put rooks on open (or semi-open) files, or behind potential "pawn break" moves.**
  The idea is to give rooks more mobility and either targets or entry points.

- **Try to get rooks to the seventh rank.**
  As the starting point of your opponent's pawns, there are not only potentially many targets on this rank, but also the possibility of cutting off and attacking the opposing king.

- **In the endgame, the king is a strong piece and belongs in the action.**
  On the average, a king's fighting power is greater than four pawns, so failing to use it is almost like accepting a four-pawn deficit!

> Always play with confidence, aggression, and respect for your opponent's moves and ideas.

- **Two connected passed pawns on the sixth rank beat a rook.**
  The two pawns can promote against a lone rook if the rook does not have any help.

- **Bishop plus a rook pawn that queens on the opposite color is a draw (assuming the defending king can get to that corner).**
  One of the few endgames where having an extra piece and pawn against a lone king is not sufficient to win.

- **A knight and a queen are usually better than a bishop and a queen.**
  That's because a bishop and a queen move similarly and thus can get in each other's way. The knight and queen move differently and coordinate better.

- **Bishops are better in open positions, knights in blocked positions.**
  Bishops are like rooks and need open lines; knights are the only piece that can "jump over" others and are thus less hindered by closed positions.

- **The bishop pair is a big advantage (about ½-pawn).**
  This occurs when one side has two bishops and the other side does not. Unless it's an unusual position like a locked board or where one or both bishops are bad, the bishop pair can be a huge advantage.

- **Rooks (of both sides) belong behind passed pawns.**
  As pawns move away from the rook, that rook gains in power and still controls the promotion square without "getting in the way."

- **An attack on the flank is best met by a counterattack in the center.**
  The center radiates throughout the entire board, so it's more difficult to ignore action there.

- **See a pawn and pick it up and all the game you'll have good luck.**
  A pawn advantage is about the difference it requires to have a theoretically winning position.

- **In middlegame positions with rooks and/or queens, move a pawn up to create *Luft* for your king and prevent back-rank mates.**
  This is especially desirable if you are not losing and don't want any sudden accidents (see also #13 above).

- **Every pawn push weakens squares – a weak square is one that can no longer be guarded by a pawn.**
  Each pawn push leaves behind squares which that pawn can no longer guard or attack. However, be wary about taking this too far, because *"You have to give squares to get squares."*

- **Don't trade off a bishop fianchettoed in front of a castled king unnecessarily, especially for pieces that are not the opponent's bishop of the same color.**
  When you push a knight's pawn up one square to fianchetto, that weakens squares around it which the bishop can guard, so it's extra sensitive to trade it unless you get your opponent's corresponding bishop, when the trade is somewhat neutral.

- **Bishops-of-opposite-color endgames tend to be very drawish, but bishops-of-opposite-color middlegames are not drawish.**
  In the endgame, it's easy with opposite-color bishops to block the opponent's pawns and achieve a draw. In the middlegame, both sides can attack on the color of the bishop they have and the opposing bishop can't defend those squares.

If you want more principles, my website www.danheisman.com has a page with a much more extensive set of principles. However, entire books are devoted exclusively to principles! For example, there are *Chess Rules of Thumb* by Lev Alburt and Al Lawrence and

The Wisest Things Ever Said About Chess by Andrew Soltis. Even more expansive is the unique book *Chess Words of Wisdom* by Mike Henebry. The subtitle of this book is *The Principles, Methods, and Essential Knowledge of Chess* – 500 pages of prose without a single diagram!

Chapter 4

//

Don't Make Lemonade When You Should Be Making Ice Tea

In all chess positions, it is important to identify your highest priorities. Unfortunately, books are full of Vladimir Kramnik games where exploiting the weak pawn on c5 is the central theme. This emphasis on positional considerations has led to far too many weak players trying to concentrate on little positional nuances when they are up or down a piece. Many guidelines deal with ideas that have very little value when compared to the value of a knight or bishop. For example, *"knight on the rim, your future is dim,"* but if you have to put a knight on the rim to win material, you should probably do so over 99% of the time!

> One of the most important principles to follow is, "Make fair trades of pieces when ahead and avoid trades if possible when behind." This does not necessarily apply to pawns.

In addition, very few books have any detailed advice on how to win when you are up large amounts of material (say, at least a piece for a pawn) because all good players learn how to do this and it is no longer of interest to them. About the only well known piece of advice given is:

LARGE ADVANTAGE GUIDELINE 1:
When ahead pieces, trade pieces.

...which is certainly good advice. I might add, *"...and don't trade pawns needlessly."* Maybe even more important is the corollary, *"When behind in material, avoid unnecessary trades of pieces"* (but if you can trade off all or almost all of the opponent's pawns, that may save you if you are down a piece or less).

However, many beginners, when way ahead – say, up a queen for a piece (a typical material imbalance!) – try to use the queen to move all around the board picking up stray pawns. Usually what happens is that they lose about 10 tempos and their opponent gets a vicious attack that wins back some of the material.

Even 1200-1400 players are not immune. Often, when they are up a piece, they are still worried about doubled or backward pawns, and end up tying up their pieces in a passive position. Or else they take the opposite tack and go too far by trying to start a completely unjustified mating attack.

So all this leads us to a guideline I think is likely more important than #1:

LARGE ADVANTAGE GUIDELINE 2:
When you are "way up" on material, take care to recognize and neutralize your opponent's "threats" and the game usually will be over.

Another way of thinking about this is to prioritize your thinking toward preventing your opponent to getting back in the game. I call this *"Think Defense First,"* which is *not* a suggestion to play passively or even "defensively," but instead to first make sure the opponent cannot do anything drastic on upcoming turns.

Consider the following position:

(see diagram next page)

Black

White
White to move

White is up a queen for a pawn and should have no trouble as long as he avoids a back-rank mate. But in this, a typical beginners' endgame position, just avoiding a back-rank mate may not be enough. Black may also be hoping to X-ray (skewer) the king to the queen or pull off some other miracle. I have seen it happen all too often.

White's best move, under high-level conditions, would be to move the queen to avoid the back-rank mate, say 1.♕b2+ followed by 2.h3 or something similar. But following Guideline 1, here is a much safer line, which I would almost always choose to play:

White	**Black**

1. ♕xd5

White eliminates the only piece that can cause him problems.

1... exd5

Now a "normal" continuation would follow the "rule" that "rooks belong behind passed pawns" and so White might try 2.♖d7, which certainly is good. However, I have also seen far too many games where allowing 2...♔e6 with tempo leads to a game where Black generates some vague counterplay with his king and his only trump, the passed d-pawn.

So White should ask himself, *"What is the only square that can hurt me?"* The answer is d1, if the black passed pawn should arrive there. But even a beginner, when asked, would see that White's king can beat Black's king to d1. So White should follow the "other" guidelines: *"The king is a strong endgame piece; centralize it and use it!"* and, *"Find your worst piece and make it better."*

2. ♔f1!

2...   **h5**

It does not really matter if Black plays this or 2...♔e6.

3. ♔e2   **♔e6 (or ♔e5)**

4. ♔d3

Black

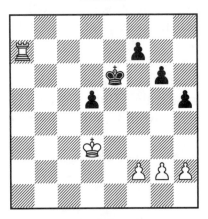

White
Black to move

There you have it – Black can do nothing. Most humans, faced with such a position as Black, understandably tend to get discouraged. I know when I play this way as White against my opponents, I can often get a quick resignation. Black just has nothing to play for, and White, simply by advancing his king up the d-file, cannot help but win while giving Black absolutely no chance to generate any dangerous counterplay.

It is worth repeating what White did. He thought:

> *I am up a queen; if I just don't get mated or lose my queen, I can win easily. **I don't really need more material. I just have to get rid of the only piece that might hurt me.** Let's see, if I take his rook and then put my king in front of the resulting passed pawn, then I wouldn't want to play Black because there would be nothing left for me to do. Now, let's calculate this again to make sure that it is really that simple... Yes, eliminate the only black piece, neutralize the pawn, and win with the rook. That is what I will do: 1.♕xd5...*

LARGE ADVANTAGE GUIDELINE 3:
The more you are winning, the more you should think defense; the more you are losing, the more you should think offense.

This concept was discussed briefly in Chapter 3 and in Guideline 1, but this advice is so important that we will look at it in more detail.

Telling the player with the better position to think defensively seems to contradict World Champion Steinitz's dictum, "When you are winning, you must attack," but it doesn't really. Steinitz was referring to positions where the material was about even but one player had the initiative, for instance due to superior development. In those cases, it is correct to attack, for passive play cannot retain the advantage as the opponent develops and time is lost.

But when one side has a large material advantage, the opposite is true. If you are up two pieces or a rook and couple of pawns, and your opponent has no compensation (say, in the form of a mating attack), then there are only a few ways you can lose:

- You can waste a lot of time moving one or two pieces while your opponent mobilizes his entire force into an attack.
- You can make large tactical mistakes, losing material back.

- You can fail to safeguard your king, letting your opponent build up mating possibilities.

- You can fail to pay attention to what your opponent is doing, thus letting him carry out threats that might not only eliminate your advantage, but actually give it to him!

So the things you should do to prevent these losing possibilities are:

- Don't waste time winning a pawn here or there. Make sure all your pieces are doing something constructive and your overwhelming force will show.

- Be extra careful and keep the position simple. You have more to lose from initiating complications. If you don't give your opponent chances, your extra material will eventually prevail.

AVOID WASTING TIME !

- Take time to safeguard your king. Make *Luft* ("air" in German) by moving a pawn up in front of your castled king, preferably creating an escape square than cannot easily be attacked by an opposing bishop.

- Pay close attention to what your opponent is doing. Ask yourself, *"What are* all *the things his move does?"* and, *"How can making that move help get him back into the game?"* and also, *"If I make any of my candidate moves, would all my pieces be safe?"*

All these factors are essentially defensive. But that is OK, since if your opponent runs out of things to do, you will eventually win without having to do anything spectacular due to your large material superiority. Here is an example of the type of tragedy that can occur when you are winning and are only thinking offense:

Black (1000)

White (1000)
Black to move

White, my student, had been attempting to checkmate Black for quite a few moves. He also had avoided several chances to trade (remember the guideline: trade pieces when ahead pieces). He was thinking "Offense, offense." There are only two ways to lose such a position: put a rook or queen in take (or lose it to a simple combination) or allow yourself to get mated. You *can't* plan on not putting your queen *en prise* (attacked but not guarded), but you *can* try to prevent yourself from being mated, so earlier trades or a timely h2-h3 to give his king *Luft* would have been proper defensive maneuvers. Now it was Black's turn, and he played:

White	Black
1...	♛b4

Now White should, as always, ask himself, *"What are all the things that move does? What can he do to me now that he couldn't do to me before?"* Instead, I watched White's eyes, which were all on Black's side of the board ("Offense, offense...").

2. ♗e8??

I was afraid of this. Black took very little time to respond and, of course, did *not* think defense by guarding his rook:

Chapter 4

2...   ♕e1 mate

You could see the physical shock go through White. White was not a very young player, but those same eyes which just a few seconds before could only see offense were now welling with tears. I tried to console him. *"It's only a game... If it hurts, that means you care and you are more likely to remember this game and be careful so it doesn't happen again. Remember, when you are winning, that is the time to think defense first."* My student recovered to win his next two games at this tournament and even to win a little money.

Now we will consider the same situation – a large material difference – from the other side. When you are losing, you should complicate, or attack. When I was a promising but still inexperienced teenager, NM Rich Pariseau told me, *"I know how to play positions when I am down a piece. I just send all my pieces after his king. If it works, I mate him; if it doesn't, I was going to lose anyway!"* Good advice!

When you are losing, you have "less to lose," so trying tricky things is more logical. If you mess up, you probably would have lost anyway. Making the position more complicated raises the standard deviation of what might happen – chessplayers call this "cheapo potential" – and makes it more likely the winning player may go wrong.

I once heard a quote, *"You shouldn't be solving problems when you play chess; you should be giving your opponents problems to solve!"* This is only common sense: the more problems you give your opponents to solve, the more likely he will fail to solve one of them and your position will improve. So if you are losing against a weaker opponent, it might make sense to make moves that would tend to make the game longer (i.e., "give him more problems to solve"), so that your opponent will have more opportunity to play worse than you do! So in that case you want to be careful not to complicate the situation in a way that is extremely favorable for your weaker opponent should he find a not-so-difficult correct move. That would tend to shorten the game, which is just the opposite of what you want to do. Just don't play too passively, else even somewhat weaker opponents find it hard to make big mistakes.

Additional guidelines for when you are far ahead in material:

- **Keep It Simple (KIS)**
Complications almost always favor the player who is losing, unless the player who is ahead is one of the world's best chess engines.

- **Don't worry about the little things**
If you are way ahead and trading queens means that you have to isolate or double your pawns, almost always trading queens is still correct.

- **Use all your pieces all the time**
This is always in play no matter what the state of the game, but especially so when you're winning. Using a hockey analogy, you are on the power play, so you would not keep your extra material on the sidelines. If you were ahead a knight but gave odds that you could never move one of your rooks, you are likely still losing!

- **Avoid unnecessary time pressure**
If you are way ahead, finding good moves is often more important than taking a lot of time to squeeze out the very best ones, since good moves should do. But you still don't want to play quickly. For example, if I had an hour left on my clock, then in a "normal" game I would aim to use almost all of my time, especially with an increment or a time delay. However, if I were way ahead I would likely play just a tiny bit faster, and aim to finish the game with about five minutes left so that I could avoid any possible "panic" time pressure blunders.

Reworking Your Priorities

It is a trait of very strong players that in materially even (or almost even) positions, they can adjust their "mental priorities" accordingly. For example, they know that when they are winning by a pawn, but have other disadvantages, such as being behind in time (development), often there are opportunities to give back the pawn and catch up in development.

But beginners learn the guidelines given in Chapter 3 and don't know how to prioritize them, not only when the position is close to even, but also when one side or the other is up a piece or more.

I sometimes ask beginners if they would weaken their kingside pawns early in the game if they could win a piece. I often use the following position, which occurred during a scholastic tournament and will be discussed further in Chapter 8:

Black (1300)

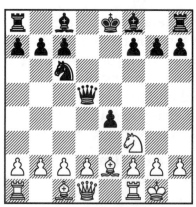

White (1180)
Position after 7...e4

Suppose White blunders with 8.♘h4? instead of 8.♘e1. With the knight on h4, I ask, *"Is 8...g5 a good move?"* I guess some even think it is a trick question (which it is not), but many, if not most, answer that 8...g5 is not a good move! I tell them that a strong player would not think twice about playing 8...g5 to win the knight – especially since they are not castled kingside. So I then ask them if we changed the position to:

(see diagram next page)

Black (1300)

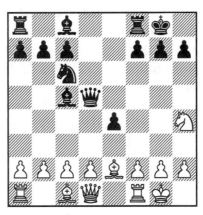

White (1180)
Hypothetical position

Would 1...g5 be a good move now? Again beginners are hesitant, but I tell them that winning a piece, in most positions, is far more important than any weaknesses caused around their king. The reasons are several, but the most important is that White does not have any pieces around Black's king to take advantage of the weakened squares and king vulnerability. And later, being up a piece, Black should have more "power" left on the board to win the fight to control the squares around his king. So Black is just winning easily after 1...g5 (not that he has a bad position without it).

It is important to note that one reason beginners tend to over-value White's chances in these types of positions is that they are used to playing more "random" chess. And the more random the game with big mistakes, the more critical it is to have the potential for disaster on bad moves – in other words, in this position the weakened king is more likely exploited if Black is a very bad defensive player than a strong player. A strong player would know that the king is not very vulnerable in this position and the reasons why; he would easily avoid the kind of moves that might allow White a strong attack. But weak players might not pay attention at all until it is too late, and then lament the winning of the knight, even if winning the knight was not the problem.

In the above example, we saw that guidelines such as, *"don't weaken your castled king position by unnecessarily pushing the pawns in front of your king,"* or *"doubled pawns are weak,"* or *"isolated pawns are weak"* are all quite secondary to the win of a knight. Sometimes there are even helpful guidelines, such as "a pawn is worth three tempos (moves)" – so if a knight is worth about three pawns, then a knight must be worth about nine tempos! Of course, it doesn't always work this way – in most positions, if you gave me nine moves in a row I would mate you even if you took off one of my knights!

All priorities are constantly shifting. Pawns that are passed, representing potential queens, become much more dangerous in the endgame, when there are fewer pieces to stop them. On the other hand, while positional guidelines become less important when one side is up material, guidelines about safety become even more important as you have more to lose. In a position where both kings are exposed to mating attacks, the most important criteria may not be who has the most pieces or pawns, but who has the first move (to start the mating attack). Just to test some students, I sometimes set up a position and ask, *"Who is better?"* without telling them who is to move! I just want them to answer, *"Whose move is it?"* And in the endgame when king *opposition* is involved, it is usually better if it is *not* your move. Take the following basic example:

Black

White
The Opposition
White to move draws; Black to move loses.

Don't Make Lemonade When You Should Be Making Ice Tea

For those unfamiliar with this theme, with White to play, a typical continuation might be: **1.♔e5 ♚e7 2.♔d5 ♚d7 3.♔c5 ♚c7** (White is making no progress with his king, so...) **4.d5 ♚d7 5.d6 ♚d8!** (5...♚c8?? loses to 6.♔c6) **6.♔c6 ♚c8 7.d7+ ♚d8 8.♔d6,** drawn by stalemate.

But with Black to move, his king must give way and White wins: **1...♚e7 2.♔c6 ♚d8 3.♔d6** (the king must lead the way!) **3...♚e8 4.♔c7 ♚e7 5.d5** and the pawn queens.

So, in many sharp middlegame positions (and endgames *not* like the one above!), having the move is often a decisive *advantage*, while in certain endgames like the one above having the move is a *disadvantage*. No wonder a chessplayer must be constantly adjusting his priorities! While these changes do make chess a more difficult game than most, it is part of the challenge that makes chess interesting and enjoyable. How many books have you seen on Tic-Tac-Toe?

Chapter 5

Know the Rules

O ne of the most important things you can do when you are learning chess is to know some of the basic rules. By this I don't
mean the way that the pieces move, but other common rules, such
as the **Touch-Move Rule:**

- **If you purposely touch a piece, you have to move it.**
- **If you let go of a piece, you have to leave it there.**
- **If you purposely touch (or displace) an opponent's piece and can take it, you must take it.**

It may sound trivial to say that a player needs to know and enforce
these rules, but I have seen the following situation occur several
times with both players unaware of the transgression:

Black (to move)

White

In this simplified version of a typical position, Black plays **1...
♖c6+**, but (properly) does not announce check. *The rules do not*

require you to announce check, although you may. You are never required to help your opponent. I teach my students not to announce check, not because it gives them some type of advantage if the opponent does not see it, but because as they improve their higher-rated opponents will be insulted *("Of course I know it is check. What do you think I am, stupid?...").* In addition, it is part of a beginning player's skill to recognize check, so why not help him learn to look at his/her opponent's moves?

Now, suppose that after **1...Rc6+** White does not closely examine his opponent's move, unfortunately a common mistake among beginners. White just sees that Black has not guarded against the threat to the knight, and therefore plays **2.Qxf4,** resulting in the following illegal position:

Black (to move)

White

At this point Black is sharp enough to know that White had to get out of check and did not, so Black says:

"Your move is illegal." [Note: At this point *Black should call the tournament director* (TD) because even many experienced tournament players don't know the proper procedure for dealing with illegal moves...]

"Why?" comes the reply from the befuddled White player, still happy over the win of the knight.

"You are in check!"

"Oh, yeah!" White now puts the knight back on f4 and the queen on e3, and instead moves his king to a safe square, say d2. Black in turn is now satisfied that justice has been done and makes another move, for instance retreating his knight to safety with ...♞g6:

Black

White (to move)
What is wrong with the above sequence?

At this point both players are happy, but Black has thrown away an easy win! What did he do wrong?

He forgot that White touched his queen! After putting the knight back on f4, Black should have declared "touch move," for then *White has to use his queen to get out of check,* losing it with 2.♕c5 or 2.♕c3. But Black was satisfied that he had called out the illegal move ruling, forgetting that touch-move also had to be applied.

As mentioned above, this type of error happens continually among beginners, and is an excellent example not only of how a simple enforcement of a known rule can have a large effect on the game, but of why the tournament director should always be called for any rule-infraction claim or unusual situation.

Chess is a Game Between Two Players...

Anyone who has seen the movie *Searching for Bobby Fischer* remembers how the parents at the scholastic tournament got locked in the school locker room. This is a slight exaggeration, but the point is clear: chess is a game between two players and the rule is that *No third party may interfere in a tournament chess game* (with some exceptions for the tournament director or cases of cheating; see also Chapter 13, "Chess Etiquette").

Even body language can be informative, and thus even unintentionally using body language to express information to a player is illegal. This prohibition on using body language not only goes for the obvious, such as a frown just as a youngster is about to touch a piece that would be a bad move, but also to the less obvious. I try not to stay any longer watching my son's game whether there is something potentially interesting or not. As a roving tournament director and master, my hovering at a board where an interesting possibility exists could tip off an astute student. For this reason U.S. Chess Federation rules stipulate that if a third party is watching a game where he has a reason to root for one of the players (such as a parent watching their child play), the spectator must watch from behind that player.

Besides Touch-Move and No Third-Party Interference, there are quite a few other rules that a beginner should know, but none is more important than: *If you don't understand what is happening at your chessboard (or you and your opponent disagree on a rule), immediately stop your clock and go ask a tournament director.* The TD may not be able to tell you what is a correct move or help you determine a checkmate, but he can tell you the definition of checkmate, stalemate, other types of draws, or pertinent rules.

I'll give two examples of this from local student play.

A few years ago, a young girl, about 10, was playing in one of our tournaments. She was doing fine and was winning by more than a queen, when she suddenly decided that continually checking with the queen (instead of using her rook to help) was the right idea. Unfortunately for her, the queen was not strong enough to do anything but continually check her opponent's king. Around and around they went. The time limit was to play the entire game in 30 minutes, and when the checking started our heroine had 10 minutes left to her opponent's 15. Her opponent was also unaware of the *threefold repetition of position* draw rule, or else decided maybe he would try to win on time. In any case, the two players continued to play the same three or four queen checks dozens of times without either making any claims or *stopping the clock to ask the tournament director* – even though they had been told many times not to let strange things happen at their board without seeking advice. I felt bad for the girl, but I was reluctant to interfere – I would directly affect the result – so I was hoping one of the players would ask me about a possible draw. Neither did. So finally the girl's clock fell and her opponent happily announced he had won on time. Understandably, the girl started to cry at the frustrating loss – when she was easily winning and even drawing – if only she had asked.

> If anything unusual happens in your game, don't argue with your opponent or guess at the rule. Stop the clock and get the tournament director.

The second incident was just as bizarre. One of my seven-year-old students was playing in a tournament where I was Assistant TD. I saw that he and his opponent were starting to put the pieces away, so I went over to ask him what happened, expecting him to say, *"I lost"* or *"I won."* Instead I got, *"I didn't want a draw!"* and tears started to well up in his eyes.

I asked what happened. Apparently his opponent had offered a draw, but had presumptuously stuck out his hand (something I teach my students not to do, as it can lead to situations like this...). My student did not want the draw, but instead of saying *"No,"* had merely shaken hands, as he had been taught by his parents that it was impolite not to shake a proffered hand. His opponent reasonably, but incorrectly, assumed that shaking hands accepted the draw offer. However, I pointed out that the U.S. Chess Federation Rulebook clearly stated that shaking hands does *not* end the game, so no draw had been agreed.

To make a long story short, after I showed his opponent the rule, he agreed to continue, but the opponent's father became upset with me for interfering with his son's game – even though I was the TD (for whom some interference is legal) and had only walked over to the game after it was apparent that the game was over: putting the pieces away is usually a dead giveaway! My student, who had been winning, finally won but, due to the misunderstanding over the rules, not everyone was happy.

Although there are hundreds of pages in the rule book, for beginners only a few rules other than those involving the pieces and the clock are required knowledge. For example, when I start teaching someone, at some point I try to make them aware of at least six types of draws:

1. Agreed draw (the most common among experienced players)
2. Threefold repetition of position (*not* repetition of moves)
3. 50-move rule
4. Both flags fallen
5. Lack of mating material
6. Stalemate

Most players are not aware of many of these draw rules, but when they are, the most common misunderstandings are:

- Mistakenly thinking that a draw is called a "stalemate." Of course, a stalemate is only one type of draw, and most draws are not stalemates.

- Mistakenly thinking that a stalemate occurs when the king has no moves. I usually point out that in the initial setup the king has no moves so, if the "no king move is stalemate" were true, the game would start as a stalemate! A good way to define it is: *A stalemate is when the player to move is not in check and has no legal move (with any of his pieces).*

- Not realizing that the 50-move rule includes 50 consecutive moves by *each player* without an *irreversible move* being made by either player. An irreversible move is a capture or a pawn move (but not castling).

- Not realizing that "threefold repetition of position" is *not* the same as both players making the same moves for three consecutive pairs of moves (such as both sides moving the same piece back and forth three times). Threefold repetition of position means that the same position has occurred (including dynamic possibilities such as castling), with the same player to move, three times during the game. It could be on moves 72, 85, and 101. Also, if only one player has the same position three times, it is not a draw! *Both* players' position must be the same – else I would try to draw with Magnus Carlsen on moves 1-5 by moving my knight back and forth! This also means that while "perpetual check" is a legitimate *concept,* it is not a draw *rule;* perpetual check will result in a draw when the same player is to move for the third time in the same position – *if* the player to move claims the draw before he moves.

- The proper way to offer a draw is to make a move, clearly state to your opponent, *"I offer you a draw,"* and then push the clock and let your opponent decide on his/her own time. The opponent may reply by stating *"I accept," "I decline,"* or may implicitly decline by making a move. Once the opponent has moved, the draw offer is off the table and the same player who offered a draw may not offer another draw until the position has changed substantially.

Among my students, both young and old, the following are the most common rules that need clarification (except for the draw misconceptions listed above):

- Promotion – most beginners seem to think that when a pawn reaches the other side of the board, you can only get back a piece that was captured! Of course, you can get a queen, rook, knight, or bishop no matter what the situation. Therefore, I commonly ask, "What is the most number of queens you can have at one time?" When the answer is "9," I know things are OK...

- Castling – All kinds of mistakes are made here:
  - The king is often not moved two squares to both sides (many like to move the king *three* squares when castling queenside). Two is always correct.
  - Similarly, some players reverse the position of the king and rook when castling (instead of moving the king two squares and putting the rook right next to the king, but on the other side).
  - Some players castle out of check or through check. Neither is legal.

Black

White
Castling through check is illegal
In this position, White cannot castle

  - Others think that you cannot castle once you have been in check. Of course, castling is still legal after you have been in check, so long as you have not moved your king or the rook with which you are castling.

- *En Passant* – many are unaware of the rule, or miss one or more of the three main ideas. I think *en passant* is best described like this:
  If a pawn moves two squares on its first move and an opposing <u>pawn</u> *could have taken it if it had only moved one square,* then the opposing pawn may

capture it just as if the pawn had only moved one square – *on the next move only.*

The key ideas (besides the *capture as if moving one square*) are: 1) The captured pawn must have moved two spaces; 2) Only a *pawn* can take it; and 3) On the next move only.

What's in a Name?

Besides "stalemate" not meaning "draw," there are other common misconceptions on chess nomenclature:

- A *knight* is not called a *horse*.

- A *rook* is not called a *castle*.

- A *forfeit* is not *resignation* (a forfeit is when someone doesn't show up for the game; a time forfeit is when a player uses more than the allotted time and is notified by the opponent). The two proper ways to resign are to clearly state "I resign" or to purposely lay down your king.

- A *tie* is not a *draw* – You can *tie for second place in a tourna-ment*, or *tie a chess match 3-3*, but you *draw* a game. By the way, if three players score 4-1 and you are next at 3-2, you did not finish second, but fourth, since there are three players with better scores than yours (this occasionally causes confu-sion by tournament participants who don't understand!...)

- A *match* is either several games played between the same players, such as a match for the world championship, or one group of players playing games on multiple boards against another group, such as the U.S. playing Russia on a four-board match in the Chess Olympiad. For some reason, some players and websites call one game between two players a "match," which is confusing.

- You *take notation* but you *record* (not "notate") a game. If you *annotate* a game, that means you write in a story of what happened (including both moves and explanations), as if it will be published in a book, magazine, or website.

- Winning *the exchange* is a chess term which means that you have won a rook for a bishop or a knight. It does *not* mean that you came out ahead in any other type of trade. For example, winning a queen for a rook is *not* winning the exchange. It does mean you came out ahead in the trade, but it would be incorrect to call it "winning the exchange." Similarly, losing the exchange means losing a rook for a bishop or knight.

- An a*ttack* (to threaten to capture *next* move) is not the same as a *capture*. And we don't *kill* pieces in chess. (It would be tough for those plastic pieces to breathe in the first place.) So next time you hear someone say, "I killed his horsey," the speaker is probably not a strong chessplayer...

- We could modify the word "tournament." Almost all the parents of my younger students initially tell me, *"Johnny is not ready for tournaments."* They picture tennis tournaments, where only the best players show up and there is immediate elimination for the losers. Nothing could be further from the truth with regards to chess. In fact, most scholastic tournaments include many beginning players.

- When beginners' parents hear the word "tournament," they immediately think *tough competition* and *elimination*. Maybe we should change the name from "tournament" to "festival." If I say, *"There is a* Chess Festival *this Saturday; why don't you bring Johnny over to play some games with the other kids?"*, I am more likely to get a positive response!

- Almost all tournaments are held in accordance with the *Swiss System,* whereby no one is eliminated – everyone plays every round – and each player is paired with someone doing as well as they are. So if a beginner starts the tournament 0-3, he will be playing someone else who's at 0-3.

- And every tournament recognizes that beginners want to compete, by giving out trophies for unrated players (those who have never played before); many now have trophies for the very low rating classes (such as Under 800, Under 600, and even Under 400) that are common among young beginners.

Chapter 6

Board Vision and Time

Which came first, the chicken or the egg?

Which comes first:

- Knowing more about analyzing and evaluating positions, which then requires you to take more time in order to move; or
- Understanding that taking more time to move is beneficial, and so you take more time and see more?

I would like to think that the second condition, the realization that taking more time is beneficial, would be the main initial cause of students playing slower (then I could get students to slow down just by telling them how beneficial it is). However, from my own experience as a beginner and as a full-time chess instructor, I would say that both of the above conditions are required for most beginners to take more time.

In my first tournaments in 1966, I was sixteen years old and the time limits were mostly 50 moves in two hours (for each player). However, initially I finished all my games in about twenty to forty minutes. I wondered why everyone was taking so long to make their moves. However, during my first three tournaments I only won one game each time – so I also realized that the other participants must have been thinking about something beneficial. As I learned more about chess – positional ideas such as the weakness of the pawn structure and transposing into bad-bishop endgames, as well as tactical ideas such as not taking a particular line of analysis for granted – I began to slow down. So there was quite a bit of the first condition in helping me take my time.

The Tortoise Always Beats the Hare...

Too fast –
Loses the thinking race

Takes his time,
But not too slow!

The key idea which I eventually realized was that I could not just wait until my opponent made a move to try to figure out what I should do. In many positions, it was possible for my opponent to make an unstoppable threat that I could not stop no matter how smart I was or how much time I took. So I learned that on each move, I had to make sure that on my *next* move I could meet all checks, captures, and threats that my opponent could reply! That takes time, and I began to play at the same pace that the other strong players did and to use almost all my time in every game.

> If you wait 'til your opponent makes an unstoppable threat, then no matter how much time you take or how smart you are, it's too late.

Many of my younger students like to play their entire game in five to fifteen minutes, no matter how much time they are given for the entire game. Other players the same age (but usually with more experience) play much more slowly. And my fast-playing students have much poorer results when playing at their normal, quick speed than they could if they played more cautiously. I call this quick playing without much consideration of the opponent's previous (much less upcoming) move, *"Flip-coin Chess."* This name implies that the aspect of skill is greatly diminished from the games when so little thought is applied – it is almost as if the two young players are flipping a coin to see who wins. It really doesn't matter that much which player has more chess knowledge, because he isn't using it! It's similar to the old term *woodpusher,* which implies a player is just pushing around the (then) wooden pieces without putting much thought into it.

For the most part, even when my students play fast and end up losing, they rarely learn their lesson and play the next game slower! This failure to learn is very interesting, and I have tried to understand what it means about human nature, my students, and my teaching methods.

For one thing, the unwillingness to slow down points out that, for many players, playing slow and thinking hard on almost every move is *work,* and *work* is less fun than *play.* You might think the more powerful emotion is that winning is more fun than losing; yet so many students would rather "play" and lose than do work and win (but not all students, thank goodness!). It also shows that simply explaining what is happening – even to bright, perceptive students – has very little impact. And age, while definitely a factor, is not the only answer – some eight-year-olds play much slower than some ten-year-olds. So what does slow down a fast player?

Peer pressure does work. If a fast player participates in a tournament with experienced players who play slow, he is much more likely to do so, too. Interestingly enough, this even works with open tournaments where young students play adults – the students not only see the benefits of playing slowly, they imitate the "group behavior" and make some attempt to take their time. Conversely, even some of my students who have learned to play slower will speed up immensely when playing against another student who plays extremely fast – usually with unfortunate results.

I try telling my students:

Playing like a jet doesn't help!

"The fates gave you your talent and the tournament director gives you time on your clock. You should use both to the maximum extent possible!"

"If you don't play slow, your rating won't grow!"

I also ask my students, *"What if you played a clone of yourself and one of you took 2-3 seconds on each move and the other took 1-2 minutes: how many games out of a hundred would the one of you playing slowly win?"*

The answer is usually 90-95%, which seems about right (this equates to about 400 USCF rating points, which is about how much strength you would lose playing five-minute versus tournament speed). I follow up by telling them that if you play fast and another student beats you 9 times out of 10, then you might be just as good as they are if you slowed down!

But since pep talks often don't work, here are some tips that may help:

- **Sit on your hands.**
  Because of the "touch-move" rule, there are absolutely no benefits to playing with your hands over the board (except in severe time pressure). So many chess coaches require their

students to literally "sit on their hands" to prevent them from reaching out and making the first move they see.

- **Pretend that the pieces are hot and heat up with each move!**
  Don't touch them until you give them a little time to cool down.

- **When you see a good move, don't play it! Instead, put it in your pocket and look for a better one.**
  This guideline is also discussed in the "Guidelines" chapter. Students seem to respond to the idea that they may have about 35 moves, on the average, in a chess position, and you are looking for the best one, not the first one your mind sees as enticing.

- **Write your moves down first, and then do a "Sanity Check."**
  After you think you have found a move, write it down, and then go back and think some more about this move from a fresh perspective, checking to see if your move is clearly crazy: *Am I just putting this piece in take? Can my opponent just take one of my pieces? Am I missing something big?* Note: writing your move first is illegal in FIDE tournaments, but is a common "alternative" rule allowed in many U.S. Chess Federation events.

- **Write down some guideline targets for time on your scoresheet before the game.**
  For example, if the tournament is Game in 90 minutes, it might be reasonable to use the "Botvinnik rule": *play the first fifteen moves in ~20% of your time.* Unless almost all of the 15 moves are "book," if you play your first fifteen moves much faster, then you are probably playing too fast. In any case, the guideline targets on your scoresheet should help remind you to pay attention to the clock. By the way, writing these time guidelines is legal, but writing analysis notes or notes about general strategy ("Speed Up!") is illegal. There is a fine line between what is illegal and what is legal, and the final discretion is up to the tournament director.

- **After your quick "book" moves, record how much time you (and your opponent, if you wish) have left after each move.**
  This can be an invaluable way of helping your chess teacher (and yourself) decide how well you are using your time. While your opponent is thinking, ask yourself, *"Am I playing too fast or too slow for this position and time situation?"* and adjust accordingly, starting next move.
  If you play a very bad move in 10 *seconds,* you are undoubtedly playing too fast. If you make the same bad move, but took 10 *minutes,* then your instructor should probably examine your general thought process to see why you would make such a bad move after careful deliberation. Writing down your time remaining every few moves is much less helpful since it becomes impossible to determine exactly which moves were played too fast or too slow.

> While your opponent is thinking, ask yourself, "Am I playing too fast or too slow for the situation?" and adjust accordingly.

It is always so gratifying for me as an instructor to see my fast students – of all ages – slow down. The smiles and results are always positive!

There once was a talented young player who played at my high school a few years after I graduated. His name was Karl Dehmelt. Even though at the time I was rated much higher than he was, I noticed something interesting: whenever there was a position where the move looked obvious, but wasn't, he would play slowly. When a position occurred where the move looked difficult, but really wasn't, he would play the correct move rather quickly. This behavior was quite the opposite of almost all the other beginning players! Others would quickly play an obvious-looking move quickly, oblivious to the potential danger.

Karl went on to become a strong FIDE Master and postal player. I, on the other hand, never forgot the lesson I learned from watching Karl's games:

Chapter 6

How much time a player takes on a move can tell you almost as much about how good they are as seeing what move they made...

I often compare the use of chess clocks with basketball referees – it's a different game without them. The element of time in chess is so important that the rules say you lose equally whether you get checkmated or use up all your time.

With the recent trend toward faster time limits and "sudden death" time controls – where all your moves have to be played before the flag falls – the emphasis on "time management" has increased. The player who uses his/her clock better has an excellent chance of winning.

> Consider your time given for a chess game
> like the time allocated for an essay test.
> Plan and adjust to use your time wisely.

In a tournament with a time control of Game in 45 minutes, one of my best students was playing another good junior player rated just below him. My student, a cautious player, took so much time for the late opening and early middlegame that he reached a complicated middlegame where he had 5 minutes left for all his moves, while his opponent had 35! His opponent was wise enough to keep the position tense, and soon thereafter my student lost material in time pressure. My student's clock management left a lot to be desired in that game. Obviously, decisions about strategy in a 2-hour game that take 3-4 minutes need to be decided in 20-30 seconds in a 30- or 45-minute game. Unfortunately, it is usually difficult to speed up complicated tactical analysis, so it is the strategic/judgment moves that must suffer (comparatively) the most to ensure that adequate time remains to keep the position "tactically even."

One final reminder: consider your time management in a chess game like taking a timed essay test: if you have the time, use almost all of it wisely!

Chapter 7

//

Just Because It's Forced...

There is an interesting type of thought-process mistake that is fairly common among players rated under 1500, although higher-rated players sometimes make it, too. This mistake occurs after the opponent makes a move that obviously responds to your threat from the previous move. You mistakenly think that just because the opponent had to make the move, that move's only purpose was to respond to your threat. Therefore, you do not take the time to look for *all* threats caused by the opponent's previous move.

In other words, you think, *"OK, he's defended my threat (or recaptured my piece); what else can I do to him?"*

A similar mistake, somewhat better but also not sufficient, would be to ask:

"Why did he make that move?"

This insufficient logic would be rectified by asking instead:

"What are all *the things my opponent's move does?"*

...because you only need to miss one thing the opponent's move does to possibly lose the game. That's why the word *"all"* has to be included in any correct question of this type.

Simply assuming your opponent is "only" responding to your threat can be a deadly mistake. It's a faulty assumption to assume that a forced move – or move that responds to a threat – cannot contain a threat itself.

The following games illustrate this mistake.

	White	Black
1.	e4	♞c6
2.	d4	e5
3.	d5	♞ce7
4.	♞c3	♞g6
5.	♝e3	d6
6.	♞f3	♝e7
7.	♛d2	♞f6
8.	0-0-0	0-0
9.	h3	a6
10.	♝d3	b5
11.	♞h2	b4
12.	♞e2	a5
13.	f4	exf4
14.	♞xf4	♞xf4
15.	♝xf4	♝a6
16.	b3	♝xd3
17.	♛xd3	♞h5
18.	♝d2	♝g5
19.	♞f3	♝xd2+
20.	♜xd2	♞f4
21.	♛e3	♛f6

Black (~1500)

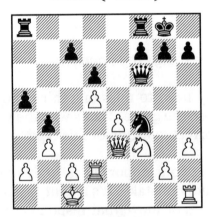

White (1400)
Position after 21...♛f6

Black has just responded to White's threat to take his knight on f4 by playing 21...♕f6. White sees that Black has guarded the knight, but stops his analysis of what Black is now threatening because he mistakenly feels the queen's only purpose in moving to f6 was to guard the knight. Of course, Black just happens to also now be threatening 22...♕a1 mate!

White proceeds to set up a pin on the knight, continuing the offensive, but completely missing any defensive idea:

22. ♖f2??

White was just completely lucky that his "offensive" move contained the defensive power of stopping the mate.

22...	**♕a1+**
23. ♔d2	**♕xh1**
24. ♕xf4	

...and Black has won the exchange (a rook for a knight).

Here is another example of a game played the same month by one of my top students:

	White (1900)	**Black (1700)**
1.	c4	c5
2.	g3	♞c6
3.	♗g2	♞f6
4.	♞c3	e6
5.	e4	♗e7
6.	♞ge2	♖b8
7.	d4	cxd4
8.	♞xd4	d6
9.	e5?	♞xe5
10.	b3	b6?
11.	f4	♞g6
12.	♞c6	♕c7
13.	♞xb8	♗b7

14. ♘b5	**♛xb8**
15. ♗xb7	**♛xb7**

Black (1700)

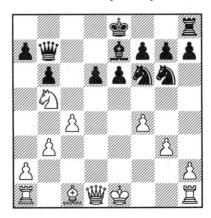

White (1900)
Position after 15...♛xb7

Black has just been forced to recapture on b7, so White, a very good player, forgets to look at his opponent's long-range threat of 16...♛xh1+. Therefore, in the game continuation, after **16.♘xd6+??** **♗xd6** White was lost as he couldn't both recapture the bishop and guard his rook.

This example brings up another point: moves that threaten across the board, especially diagonal moves, are easy to miss. You have an excuse in a speed game, but in slower chess sometimes you just have to "look around."

The following diagram is yet another example of this chapter's theme:

(see diagram next page)

Black (1100)

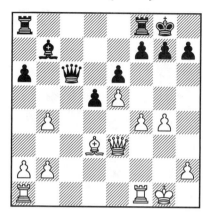

White (1500)
Position *before* 1...d4

Black so far has played a nice game against his much higher-rated opponent. He now correctly opens the long diagonal with **1...d4,** threatening both 2...dxe3 and mate on g2. White was expecting this move and played **2.♕h3,** defending the mate, but also...

Black thought for a while and played **2...♕h1+??.** An old principle is, *"Always check, it might be mate!"*, but it is not really a very good guideline, and this is an example! After **2...♕h1+??** White is forced to play **3.♔f2,** threatening the queen on h1 *and* the mate on h7. Black, who had not seen the mate on h7 because he thought the move 2.♕h3 was only made to save the queen and guard g2 (mate on h7 was the *third* thing 2.♕h3 did...), now retreated his queen from h1 and was surprised when he was mated with **4.♕xh7 mate.**

It is important to note that board-vision problems are not limited to the young, only the young at heart (or at least those without too much chess experience!). In the next example, my student is retired, but he falls prey to the same problem my younger students exhibited above.

Black (1100)

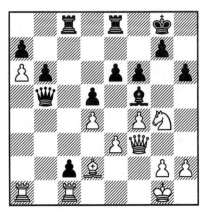

White (1400)

In this position, Black has lost a piece for two pawns against a higher-rated opponent, but the game is not over. Having just driven the knight out of e5 with ...f7-f6, he feels compelled to attack it again:

White	Black
1...	h5?!
2. ♘f2	e5?

Black reasoned, *"I know why the knight went to f2; it was to avoid capture with the pawn I just attacked him with."* As the reader knows by now, a move that was forced may also contain a threat. White of course played...

3. ♕xh5

...and went on to win.

This brings up another important point. The move 2.♘f2 is a discovered attack by the queen on the h4-pawn. Inexperienced players have a tendency to look only at what the moving piece does on its destination square, often overlooking other aspects of the move such as:

- discoveries (for bishops, rooks, and queens of either side),
- line blocks (again for bishops, rooks, and queens of either side),
- removing guards,
- things the moving piece is no longer doing on its previous square, and
- leftover threats from the previous move, etc.

Here is yet another example of the "just because it is forced" mistake from a tournament game between two of my students:

Black (1100)

White (1100)

White is lost, as Black is skewering his knight and e-pawn. However, at this level anything might happen, so he tries to counterattack:

White	Black
1. ♜e2	♞g4

Black's knight is attacked, so he retreats it to the most reasonable square. Naturally, but incorrectly, White is not worried about the offensive aspect of such an obvious retreat...

2.	♘b5??		♖c1+
3.	**Resigns**		

It is mate on the back rank on the next move, as the "retreat" **1....♘g4** also covered the white king's only escape square, f2. White could have saved the knight and covered the threat with 2.♘c2 or 2.♘f3.

In the above examples, the defender was simply making a forced move and was "lucky" that his opponent made the mistake of not looking for other threats that the forced move created as a by-product. However, the astute player can also consciously use the tendency of his opponent to overlook the offensive threat of defensive-looking moves. Here is a cute example from one of my games:

White	**Black**
Opponent (1700)	Dan Heisman

	White	Black
1.	e4	c5
2.	♘f3	e6
3.	♘c3	♘c6
4.	b3	d5
5.	exd5	exd5
6.	♗b5	♘f6
7.	0-0	♗e7
8.	♘e5	♕c7
9.	♖e1	♗e6
10.	♗b2	0-0
11.	♗xc6	bxc6
12.	♕f3	♖fe8
13.	♘e2	d4
14.	♘f4	♗d5
15.	♘xd5	cxd5
16.	c3	dxc3
17.	♕xc3	d4
18.	♕h3	♗f8
19.	♘f3	♕f4
20.	♕h4	

My opponent is rated much lower than me and is playing for a draw. So far, I have done nothing to demonstrate why I have a higher rating, but over the next few moves I show signs of thinking.

20…	♕f5
21. ♗a3	h6

When playing 21…h6, which defended against some later ♘f3-g5 threats, I began to notice that my opponent's queen was awkwardly placed. Unfortunately, there was the problem of completely ensnaring the queen by covering all the escape squares. I then realized that if my opponent continued to attack the "backward" c-pawn, I might be able to make the rare "offensive" defensive move.

22. ♖ec1

Heisman

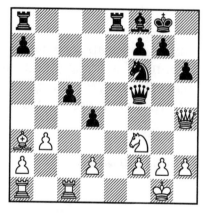

White (1700)
Position after 22.♖ec1

22…	♖ac8!

This is it! While apparently overprotecting my c-pawn, I create a deadly threat. I actually made this move rather quickly so that my opponent would think I was just responding to his pressure on the c-pawn. (Note to readers who like to computer check: The engine says I could have played 22…g5 immediately and don't necessarily need this preparatory move. However, using this game and move does fit the purpose of our chapter!)

23. ♖c4?

...which my opponent, somewhat justifiably, misses.

23...	g5!
24. ♕g3	♘e4

> ## What are *all* the things my opponent's move does?

The door is shutting. The apparently innocuous 22...♖ac8 covered the crucial c7 escape square. So White is forced into...

25. ♕h3	g4
26. ♘h4	♕xf2+
Resigns	

The conclusion from all of the above examples (and many more not shown – this is a common mistake!) is the same: Whether you are an experienced player or not, you always must be aware that *your opponent's move often does more than just its seemingly main purpose* – so be on your guard!

"What are all the things my opponent's move does?"

Assume the Best

Let's return to the following position, first addressed in Chapter 4:

Black (1300)

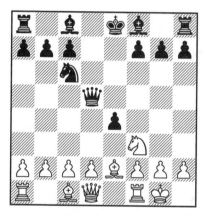

White (1180)
Position after 7...e4

This position was reached after the moves **1.e4 e5 2.♘f3 ♘f6 3.♘c3 ♘c6 4.♗e2(?) d5 5.exd5 ♘xd5 6.♘xd5(?) ♕xd5 7.0-0(?) e4.**

Up to this point, White has made several small mistakes: he met Petroff's Defense with the passive (though acceptable) 3.♘c3; he chose the least aggressive post for his bishop with 4.♗e2(?); in trying to avoid doubled pawns, he brought Black's queen powerfully to the center with 6.♘xd5(?); finally, he erred by allowing Black's e-pawn to advance by playing 7.0-0(?).

In this position an experienced player would reason thus:

"My knight is attacked and I have no worthwhile counterattack, as 8.c4!? would create weaknesses on d3 and d4 in return for very little, and my problem with my knight would still not be resolved. 8.♘h4 seems to lose a piece to the 'attack it with something worth less (AWL)' move 8...g5, where the weakening of Black's kingside is trivial compared to my loss of a piece. 8.♖e1 temporarily sets a trap that works if he takes my knight with 8...exf3?? 9.♗xf3+ winning Black's queen, but since he doesn't have to take the knight next move, if he just plays safe with a move like 8...♗e7, then I will lose my knight. Therefore, I should play 8.♘e1."

White, who at that time was a promising but raw tactical player who primarily had played weaker opponents, went through the first part of this analysis, but stumbled when he considered 8.♖e1. Accustomed to facing opponents who routinely fell into traps, White apparently thought:

"The retreat 8.♘e1 is to be avoided, if possible. I will set a trap by playing 8.♖e1; if he plays 8...exf3?? then 9.♗xf3+ wins the queen! Then I won't have to retreat my knight."

The problem with this logic is that it assumes the opponent won't make the best move! This dangerous thinking sometimes works if the opponent is very weak or if his best move is very difficult to find, two conditions that exist a lot less often than many players would think! In the above game, Black was actually the better player (which White knew, from their ratings). Black thought for only about ten seconds to decide on his reply; after all, even if he hadn't seen the trap beforehand, it is not difficult to say to oneself,

"He is leaving a knight en prise! *What will happen if I just take it? I lose to a check! So I will just stop the check and his knight will have no place to go!"*

After 8.♖e1?, Black played 8...♗e7 and *then* White went into a deep think – too late! Black has won the knight, and he won the game easily.

White, partly through the bad experience of this game, quickly came to realize that he would play quite a bit better if he assumed his opponent would find the best reply. As a teenager, he was better equipped to handle the lesson learned from the above example.

Very young children (usually, 7 and under), however, often have trouble considering their opponents' moves (unfortunately some older folks have this problem, too...). The young child makes easily parried "threats," reasoning that, *"I will go here to threaten his queen and, after my opponent makes a move, I will take it off!"*

The youngster assumes that their opponent, like themselves, will ignore *their* opponent's (the youngster's) moves, and that any threat is reasonable as it is likely to get ignored by the other player and thus executed on the following move. This faulty logic is reinforced by other young beginners who, using the same faulty logic, make it come true!

A game between beginners is often characterized by both sides making gratuitous threats, no matter how silly or easily met, because the chances of great rewards from the opponent missing the threat are too good to resist.

Unfortunately, when faced with more experienced opponents, the beginner often just loses material as his/her "threat" is easily met. For example, their opponent might just be able to capture the piece which was threatening their queen. Other unwise threats might just lose tempos or misplace pieces in the hope that the opponent will overlook that threat.

In the above example of a player meeting a threat to his queen by just capturing the attacking piece, it was not enough that an opponent's piece was unsafe on the *next* move if the opponent could capture the attacking piece *this* move. Inexperienced players do not have the board vision, the experience, or (often) the patience to check to see if all their moves and pieces are safe. Their sophistication of play and playing strength would increase immensely if they just checked their opponent's last move and asked:

Chapter 8

"What are all *the things that move does?"* or:

"What are all the things my opponent can do next move if I don't move at all?"

– and didn't start thinking about their reply until they at least came to some reasonable answer. Sometimes the answer is, *"My opponent has blundered!"*

As a positive side effect, assuming that your opponent will make his best moves causes you to play slowly! For each move that you are considering (and to find the best move, you must seriously consider any reasonable move), you cannot judge how good the resulting position is unless you figure out what your opponent is likely to do. This task can range from trivially easy *("...there is only one way he can get out of check...")* to enormously difficult, depending upon the position and the opponent. But one thing is clear: until a beginning player learns to attempt to do this on *every* move, he will consistently be defeated by opponents who do.

To show you how important it is to assume best moves in order to correctly evaluate a position, consider the following silly counter-example. Suppose Magnus Carlsen is playing Fabiano Caruana, and Carlsen is up a pawn with a good position, and it is his move. Further suppose someone asks me, *"Who do you think is winning?"* Would it make any sense for me to answer, *"Carlsen is up a pawn with a good position, but Caruana is winning because I think Carlsen is going to put his queen in take!"?!* No? But that kind of illogic is what happens when you do *not* assume that best play will happen for the purpose of evaluating a position.

From the above discussion (and other discussions in this book), we can conclude that in order to play "non-beginning" chess, a player has to at least do the following:

- **Take time** to figure out why the opponent made his move, what threats created by that move (or left over from the previous moves!) may have to be parried, and what are *all* the things the opponent could do to you on the next move if you are not careful.

- **Try to visualize** possible moves *before* finally touching a piece to move it.

- **Make sure that *all* your pieces are safe** before you move (*"Can I meet all my opponent's checks, captures, or threats that he can reply to this move?"*), and if your opponent's pieces are not safe, that you *consider* their capture.

- **If you see a good move, put it in your pocket and look for a better one.** You are trying to find the best move you can in a reasonable amount of time.

- **Assume the opponent will make the best reply,** and try to figure out for any of your moves under serious consideration what the opponent's reply would likely be (and whether the opponent's reply might create a threat that cannot be parried).

The first four above are absolutely mandatory to move past the beginner stage. The fifth is a little more sophisticated, but still absolutely essential for any serious progress.

The Three Levels of Chess Thought

The above discussion touches upon some problems that beginners have in their thinking process. The following examines this phenomenon in more detail.

Some years ago a student, rated 1100, played in a tournament in which his playing strength was 1900 (!) for six rounds. He beat four players rated higher than anyone he had ever beaten before.

As a full-time chess instructor, I was very intrigued about what had caused this sudden great jump in playing strength. Could it be attributed to random chance or just "having a good tournament"? After some thought and discussion with the student, I came up with a theory that is based on the following three types of thought processes. The ascent through these processes reflects the maturing of a chessplayer:

Chapter 8

Flip-Coin Chess

In Flip-Coin Chess a move is played quickly and without serious thought. The winner of a game where both players are playing Flip-Coin Chess is almost random, and thus I named it after a coin flip. If one player plays Flip-Coin Chess and the other actually takes time to think and consider his opponent's last move and alternative candidate moves, the thoughtful player almost always wins. Flip-Coin players don't use the principle, "If you see a good move, look for a better one." They just usually play the first "good" one they see, even if it's not really so good. Almost all young beginners (and some older ones) start by playing Flip-Coin Chess.

Hope Chess

One step up from Flip-Coin Chess is Hope Chess. Hope Chess is *not* when you make a move and hope your opponent doesn't see your threats or when you make a bad move and hope your opponent does not punish it (although this concept has been erroneously described these ways many times since I first proposed it).

Hope Chess (by my original definition) is when you make a move and don't anticipate all your opponent's dangerous moves that he can make in reply to your candidate moves. Dangerous moves are always forcing moves: checks, captures, and threats. Then, when your opponent does make such an unforeseen threat next move, you think, *"Uh-oh! I hope I have an answer for this."* Often the answer is, *"Too late! No matter how smart you are or how long you think, there is no defense against that threat."*

> Dangerous moves are always forcing moves: checks, captures, and threats.

Good players don't play this way, else anyone could beat them just by making a threat that cannot be met. Obviously this does not happen very often, and the reason is that good players don't wait to see if they can meet threats; they only make a move if they are sure that no matter what check, capture, or threat the opponent may reply, they are ready with a safe and good answer discovered on their previous move. This takes time, and that's one reason why good players always play slowly and carefully.

In my first three tournaments, I unknowingly played Hope Chess and did not win more than one game in any of the three events! It also partly explains why I played so quickly, since *not* looking at what might happen next move removes much of the need for critical thought.

Real Chess

The "good" thought process that was described above for strong players, I call "Real Chess." When a good player considers a candidate move, he asks, "What are all the dangerous replies to this move and how would I meet them?" If he discovers that there are no good ways to meet a certain reply to a candidate, then he often has to reject that candidate and consider only other moves. In playing Real Chess, you either choose candidate moves that you analyze as being safe on all replies, or maybe purposely choose one that is technically "not safe" but is instead a reasonable sacrifice. But in either case, you do your very best on the previous move not to be surprised by a threat that cannot be met on the next move.

One goal of Real Chess is to anticipate each of your opponent's dangerous replies. If he makes a dangerous move that you had not even considered, that is not a good sign! This anticipation takes some time and real effort, so it's not surprising that if you go to a chess tournament, the last players to finish are usually the best players!

It only takes one bad move to lose the game. Let's make an analogy. Suppose you build a house where the temperature is -20°F outside. You settle on a one-room design with four walls, a floor, and a ceiling. However, you decide to save a little on materials by only finishing half the ceiling. Even though you have constructed over 90% of the structure, with only half a roof the temperature will still be about -20°F inside. If you want your heater to be effective, you need to enclose the entire house.

Chapter 8

This "cold house" analogy is what happens when you play Real Chess only 90% of the time. In a 40-move game, that is only 36 safe moves, and anything might happen on the other four. Even 95% leaves two moves that could easily lose the game. So Real Chess is only truly played when you do it on every move, not just most or almost all of them.

This very much explains how my 1100-rated student made such a large leap. He knew about playing Real Chess but had never really conscientiously done so game after game. However, he was playing in a team event with my son and some other friends, and he had resolved he was going to try his best on every move, not just most of them. Finishing that last part of the roof made a gigantic difference!

It's easy not to do this. In 1998 my son Delen, then 15, was playing in the Under 1400 Section of the World Open. He won his first four games and was doing well until the seventh round. He was paired with a 1300 player and was outplaying him up and down the board for the first 50 moves, and had an easily won endgame, ahead the exchange (rook for bishop or knight) plus a couple of extra pawns.

At that point Delen's opponent checked him and, even though he was not in time trouble, he *immediately* moved his king to a square where his opponent could knight-fork his king and rook!

Dad almost had a heart attack! *"How can you play like an 1800 player for 50 moves and then like a 400 player for one, throwing the entire game away?!?"* The reply was pure "young Delen":

"I can't work hard on every move; it's too much effort!"

Agh! This is similar to working hard on a painting for three weeks and then, in a quick fit, suddenly throwing paint all over it. Once the damage is done...

So the difference between what Delen did and my formerly 1100 student is clear. The 1100 worked hard on every move and got the desired results. In that World Open, Delen only worked hard on most moves and got the deserved results.

My explanation of what happened to my student is now more than a guess. From talking with that student and subsequent students over the years, I have found that Real Chess (and the Real Chess barrier, which is about a 1700 USCF/FIDE rating) is an explanation as to why many otherwise decent chessplayers get stuck around that level. It's an insight I was proud to make and publicize. The first article I wrote on this idea was called, "The Secrets to Real Chess."

Can this "secret" take you from 1800 to 2400? Of course not. As any high-rated chessplayer knows, there is a lot more to playing good chess than just trying hard, taking your time, and making sure your moves are safe. But *not* playing Real Chess can keep your rating below 1700-1800 forever, so it's necessary (though not sufficient) to achieving high-level play.

Chapter 9

//

Don't Believe Him!

When playing a high-rated player, there is sometimes an amount of "bluffing" that may occur. Your opponent may offer a sacrifice that may or may not be sound and you have to use your judgment as to whether you should take the material.

Closer to beginner level, the problem is somewhat reversed.

Opponents are always making mistakes, and a player needs to recognize these mistakes. Sometimes there is a tendency to treat a lower-rated player like a much stronger player. Often, I see games between two lower-rated players where one player offers material based on some miscalculation and his opponent declines to take it, feeling that if someone is offering something for free, it can't be good! Of course, in many cases, it is just a blunder and you should take it, saying (to yourself) *"Thanks!"*

Black (1350)

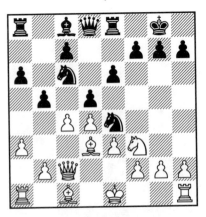

White (1400)
Position after 11...b5?

Don't Believe Him!

In the above position, Black has just responded to White's threat to capture on e4 with **11...b5?**. Now it is true that ...b7-b5 still allows a strong capture on e4: **12.♗xe4 dxe4 13.♕xe4 ♗b7** as in the game when White should continue 14.cxb5 axb5 (or 14...♘a5 15.♕g4) 15.♕g4 with advantage. However, there is no reason to believe that Black's move is a good counterattack. The even simpler 12.cxb5 axb5 13.♗xb5 attacks Black's knight and leaves White with the bishop pair (when one side has both bishops and the other does not) and a solid passed a-pawn.

After the game, I asked White why he didn't simply take the b-pawn. He replied that he believed Black's threat and thought that the black rook would be able to menace his queenside (in Benko Gambit fashion) from b8. I call such groundless fears "Phantom Threats."

It seems that the ability to differentiate between real and phantom threats is a strong problem with players in the 800-1600 rating range.

Phantom threats occur because of laziness or haziness. An inexperienced player does not try to logically calculate all the possibilities. Instead, he takes "shortcuts" in thinking, like *"my opponent's queen may try to get me. So maybe I will move up that pawn so the queen cannot go there."* In doing so, the beginner doesn't actually calculate whether or not the opponent's move is reasonable, or even a real threat. He just decides to come up with a rationale for a move, and convinces himself that the move is the best one without any real analysis.

When there is a position that calls for careful analysis but a weaker player just rationalizes or uses principles instead of careful calculation, I call this *"hand-waving."* Hand-waving is not only lazy, but in the long run quite dangerous. You don't get to be good at analysis by not practicing it when it is needed!

When I ask a low-rated player to think out loud, they almost always include quite a bit of "hazy" thinking. They don't try to systematically look at the opponent's checks, captures, or threats (the forcing moves) from the previous move. They don't always strongly consider all of their own checks, captures, or threats, either. Because of this, they often "believe" their opponent's last move and respond to it whether or not it made any sense or carried any real threat. More experienced opponents, when playing inexperienced players, never "believe" their opponent's move – they check the variations themselves to see if maybe the opponent just gave them something for free or if their threats are ignorable. It may be possible that allowing a "threat" may be good for them, and not their opponent!

Here is a typical example from a game by one of my students:

Black (1050)

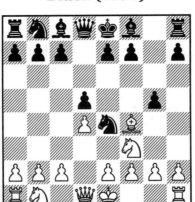

White (1150)

My student is playing White and Black has just played **4...g5?**. I am so accustomed to looking at these types of strange moves with my beginning students that I expected White to play almost anything except the obvious and good 5.♘xg5. I have seen so many 500-700 level players respond to a move like 4...g5 by retreating the bishop that I have almost come to expect the non-logical retreat.

There are two reasons these lower-rated players give to justify the bishop retreat. It is either, *"My bishop is attacked by a pawn that is guarded; therefore I must retreat or lose the bishop;"* or,

Don't Believe Him!

"If I take the pawn, then he will trade off my bishop (knight), and I don't want to trade."

They don't see the capture as just a series of exchanges that win a pawn. Moreover, lower-rated players almost always take with the bishop, because that is the attacked piece. Giving up the bishop pair (worth about ½-pawn bonus according to GM Larry Kaufman) for no reason is not correct. However, in this case White, rated 1150 and not 650, did just what he should have and played 5.♘xg5. I was somewhat surprised!

For players with *very* low ratings, it is usual not to even look at or calculate your opponent's threats. For example, I have seen the following type of position a thousand times (or so it seems!) in beginners' games:

Black

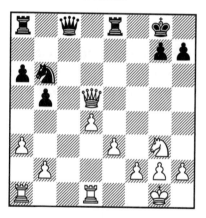

White

White has just played his queen to d5 and announces "check"! Black hears that dreaded call and "sees" that indeed, the line between the queen and his king indicates his king is in danger (a "check"), so immediately out comes his/her hand to touch the king. Then, after grabbing it, comes the pause as Black decides onto which square the king should move. In other words, they believe that White has made a (safe) fearsome move, and immediately react defensively.

Afterward, I set up the position again and ask Black, *"What are the three ways to get out of check?"*

> ## You can't play what you don't see.

Black will often dutifully reply, *"Move the king to a safe square, put something in the way, or take off the piece that is checking you."*

I then ask, *"Of those ways, which do you think might often be the best?"*

To this question, they *will* think and answer, *"I guess taking off the piece."*

"Well, in this position what do you think is the best way to get out of check?"

Faced with the reality of their previous replies, eyes will now wander over the board as if seeing the position for the first time, and those same eyes will undoubtedly discover that the checking queen could have been removed for free by the knight on b6. So out comes the sheepish reply, *"I guess ♘xd5."*

"Then why didn't you take the queen instead of moving your king?" I know the answer, but I want the youngster to think about what he did, so as to better remember and not repeat the mistake.

A quiet voice replies with a smile, *"I guess I didn't see it."*

*"You have to look. And that requires being careful and taking time. After all, **you can't play what you don't see.**"*

Chapter 10

//

The Three Big Areas For Improvement

Many beginners make chess way too difficult. They pick up advanced texts full of grandmaster games and believe that the subtle strategies that grandmasters use to get the advantage against one another are the secret to their own improvement. Actually, working on those subtle strategies could delay your improvement quite a bit by deflecting your concentration onto the wrong issues, just as it would hurt your progress in math if you tried to learn geometry before you learned to count or add.

As Michael de la Maza, author of the book *Rapid Chess Improvement,* once wrote to me,

"I read Silman's book How to Reassess Your Chess *[DH: a very good, but advanced book on positional evaluation and planning] and it had many things I did not know, so I thought, 'This is it!.' So in the next game I spent a lot of time trying to get a good knight versus a bad bishop but then I lost my knight!"*

As it turns out, there are three areas that most beginning (and some not-so-beginning!) players need to work on to get to a good intermediate level:

- **Safety/Tactics** – Most players learn to spot fairly easy offensive tactics, but almost none spend much time learning how to prevent those tactics from happening to them. Both offensive (winning) and defensive (preventing from losing) tactics are very important.

- **Time Management** – Serious chess is always played with a clock, and playing too fast or too slow for the entire game can be disastrous. Moreover, spending too much or too little time on the wrong moves can be equally disastrous.

- **Piece Activity** – "Use all your pieces all the time": this idea seems simple, but almost all beginners (and many non-beginners!) have trouble implementing it in practice.

Safety/Tactics

To illustrate the point of how safety dominates chess, there is a computer chess engine that plays online that has been "dumbed down" to play against intermediate players. The programmer fixed the engine so that it could only look four ply (two moves) ahead. In other words, from the start of the game it could not look further than 1.e4 e5 2.♘f3 ♘c6. Beyond that, it is blind. Moreover, the engine has fairly little strategic finesse. What do you think is its rating?

Turns out the computer plays at a level comparable to FIDE/USCF 1650! That's stronger than the average adult tournament player! What does this mean?

It means that tactics – especially basic, easy, tactics – dominate chess playing strength. As GM Alexey Shirov wrote, "I have come to believe that these easy tactics are the basis for everything."

As I wrote above, it's not just finding easy tactics that win material; most players start to get good at that with some tactics practice. Almost every tactics book is written to help the reader develop his "Play and Win," "Play and Draw," or "Play and Mate" offensive capabilities. *However, it's just as important, if not more so, to have the capability to see whether your move is safe,* i.e., to prevent basic tactics from being played against you. Most players are not nearly so good at the ability to check to see if their moves are safe, but they need to be in order to become a decent player. It's one reason I wrote my most recent, but fairly advanced, book *Is Your Move Safe?*.

So, sure – the grandmaster games are often decided by subtle positional maneuvering to get the advantage followed by clever tactics to take advantage of the superior position. But that's not necessarily the goal of much weaker players. If they can just start by consistently making safe moves and recognizing when the opponent's moves are not safe, then even a modicum of basic strategic ideas is more than sufficient to make those weaker players stronger than most intermediates! That's an important lesson to learn.

> Relying on your tactical vision alone, without also using analysis to determine safety, is a common source of unsafe moves.

In my experience, when two players rated under 1500 face each other, there's about a 99% chance that one of them will allow the opponent an easy tactic at some point. For example, it could be a tactic about on par with those that appear in Bain's *Chess Tactics for Students* book.

Here are two examples I often use:

Black to move. Is 1...♛xb5 safe?
Black

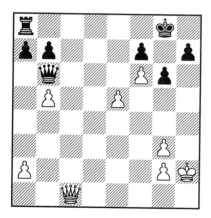

White

The answer is No. If Black plays 1...♛xb5, then White replies 2.♛h6 with the unstoppable threat of 3.♛g7 mate next move.

There are two very important things to learn from this simple problem:

- If you are not careful, it's very easy for your opponent to generate unstoppable threats. So if you just move and wait to see what your opponent does, and he makes a check, capture, or threat (the forcing moves), it may be that there is no answer. Therefore, in slow games, if you want to become a good player, you have to check on each candidate move to make sure your opponent has no such unstoppable threat in reply. If he does have such a threat, and you don't wish to sacrifice, then you may have to reject that candidate move. It only takes one bad move to lose the game.

- Most of my students, when given this problem, agree that they have seen similar mating patterns before, and this helped them to solve the problem correctly. That means that the study of basic tactics (in this case the easy mating pattern around the black king) is very helpful, even necessary. However, there are many fairly simple patterns that are not commonly found in basic tactics books, so using your *tactical vision should enhance your analysis, not replace it.* Sometimes only careful analysis will find a safety issue, so *depending on your tactical vision alone is not sufficient.* Often my students only use their tactical vision and, when they allow an easy tactic, say *"I did not see that!"* and what they mean is that they only looked for a recognizable pattern; they did not take the time to carefully analyze the safety of their move.

White to move. Is 1.♘c3 safe?
Black

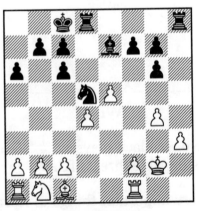

White

The answer is No. If 1.♘c3, Black can reply 1...♘b4, and White cannot defend both the discovered attack by the rook on the d4-pawn and the direct attack of the knight against c2, a double threat. White will lose at least a pawn.

This problem proved to be much more difficult for my students than the previous one, even though both are answered by unstoppable one-move threats. One of the main reasons most students get this problem wrong is that the pattern 1...♘b4, unlike the previous problem, is not a well-known dangerous pattern in similar positions. So while the previous problem can be solved "by examination" and recognition of the danger to the black king, this problem requires careful analysis instead, which in general is both more work and more foreign to lower-rated players.

> Not all of the things that are considered
> bad for your position are equally bad!

I have given both of these problems to hundreds of students and the contrast is quite stark – the first problem is "easy" and the second one proves much more challenging. I often hear that 1.♘c3 is not a good move, not because 1...♘b4 wins a pawn, but because Black can double White's pawns with the innocuous 1...♘xc3 2.bxc3. This exchange, and the resultant doubled pawns, are easy to see, but pale in comparison of the real answer 1...♘b4.

As a side note, I might add that inexperienced players seem more afraid of doubled pawns than they are of many more important issues, like trading pieces when behind. The same player who would go out of his way to avoid doubled pawns would think nothing of needlessly trading a piece or three when behind in material, even though the latter transgression is usually far more likely to result in defeat. It's easy to know that losing a rook is worse than losing a pawn, but it takes a lot more experience to realize that *unnecessarily trading down when losing is much worse than accepting doubled pawns*. Not all bads are equal!

Chapter 10

Time Management

Like the proper way to take an essay test, the right idea in a chess game is to use almost all of your time. This is equivalent to trying the best you can. In a two-hour essay, you would not scribble down a couple sentences and hand in your paper in five minutes. But neither would you leave your paper blank until the last two minutes and then try to write a decent 4-5 page essay in 120 seconds. The right approach is to use the full two hours to write the best essay you can.

Similarly, in chess if you play too slowly, you get into unnecessary time pressure and make hasty mistakes at the end. Play too quickly and you play less than your best and make hasty mistakes all along. The right approach is to pace yourself all along and use just the right amount of time to optimize your play. I call this the *Goldilocks Principle,* and apparently this idea of naming things "Goldilocks" for not going to extremes has been used in other endeavors than porridge temperature and chess.

Sure, if your opponent falls into an opening trap and resigns, you won't use all your time; in fact, in this rare case you may use very little. But the intention should be to use almost all your time every game, assuming your game goes a "normal" number of moves (you can assume about 40 when the game starts and then adjust accordingly depending on the types of positions that arise).

One way to help do this is to write down your time remaining after every move (well, maybe after every move after you finish making your "book" opening moves quickly). This makes you aware of your time usage. Then, while your opponent is thinking, you can ask yourself the crucial question:

"Am I playing too fast for the situation or too slow?"

...and react accordingly. If you are playing too fast, then you can start taking more time, especially on complicated and critical moves. If you are playing too slowly, then you can start to pick up the pace, especially moving faster on "judgment" moves where intense calculation is not necessary and the game does not hang in the balance.

The goal would be to try to keep on course toward playing at about the correct pace. You don't want to move too slowly and then realize, as your clock is ticking down toward zero that, all of a sudden, you need to move much faster. Correcting your time only at the last moments is often disastrous. Nor would you want to play too fast and then, just before you resign, realize that you could have taken an extra 40 minutes on your earlier moves to prevent the current disaster.

In general, you want to *use your time to avoid getting into trouble,* not play fast and then save your time for getting out of trouble.

Besides using all your time wisely (I call this "Macro Time Management"), there is another aspect to the good use of your time: allocating it to moves (and thus positions) that deserve it. As an easy example, you would not spend as much time on the first move of the game (certainly a "book" move) than you would on a complicated position where the entire outcome of the game is likely riding on that move. The ability to differentiate between moves that require careful attention and those that can be played relatively quickly without much risk is called "Criticality Assessment."

When you are playing, there is an average amount of time you want to take on each move. For example, if the game is a 90-minute contest and we assume you have about 40 moves in a game, that's 90/40, or 2 minutes and 15 seconds per move. If there is also a 10-second time increment, then you have 2 minutes and 25 seconds per move.

But clearly you don't want to aim to spend about the average time on each move. If you have a "book" opening move or only one safe recapture, then those moves should be played relatively quickly, leaving time for moves that require more than the average. As stated above, the moves that require more than the average time are critical moves like complicated positions, or decisions on whether to trade into a king-and-pawn endgame.

I have noticed that some of my students are very careful, but when the position gets complicated they get overwhelmed and feel that they cannot get a good result when taking time to calculate carefully. Thus, ironically, they end up playing fairly slowly when the position is non-critical ("Where should I develop my bishop?") and fairly quickly when it is complicated ("Let me just take that rook and see what happens"). I call this syndrome, "Playing Chess Backwards" because they are taking time when they should not, and not taking time when they should.

It's true that if you don't have the requisite skills (visualization, chess logic, pattern recognition) to analyze carefully, you probably won't do well even if you do take time on complicated moves. However, while practice doesn't make perfect, practice does make "much better," so avoiding practicing visualization and careful analysis will just mean that you will remain weak in those skills. Instead, whether it is puzzles or complicated positions, taking time to carefully analyze the position is a learned skill, and the more you do it, the better you will become.

As a final note on analysis, whenever possible you should analyze positions and games with strong players. Listen to what they are doing (and what they are not doing), how they are doing it, what moves they consider, the order of the moves, how often they come back to previous lines, how and when they evaluate positions, and which moves interest them. All of these skills are much more quickly developed when you have a role model on whom to base your thought process.

Activity

"Use all your pieces all the time."

In a basketball game, the team is allowed 5 players on the court, so at the start of the game the coach always puts out 5 before he runs any plays. The same thing is true in any team sport – all teams use the maximum number of players allowed. Yet for some reason beginning chessplayers, who are the "coach" of their team, don't put all the players they can on the court before trying to run any plays!

The Three Big Areas for Improvement

How can they get away with that?

Because their weak opponents are doing the same thing, so the game is competitive.

But what happens when the opponent is developing his pieces more efficiently?

Many years ago I wrote a "Novice Nook" column titled "Chess Master vs. Chess Amateur" (named after the well-known book by Dr. Max Euwe and Walter Meiden) where I presented five games I played in one evening against a much weaker player. Those games were all characterized by the same thing: I developed as many pieces as possible early in the game and my opponent made many time-wasting moves like ...h7-h6. Soon my lead in development was overwhelming and I won all five games in fewer than 20 moves each.

The three main *goals* of the opening are to develop all the pieces, try to control the center, and find a safe place to tuck the king for the middlegame (castle!). However, a principle differs from a goal in that a goal is something you are trying to achieve, while a principle is a heuristic ("saying," "guideline") which tells you how to do something, or how to do it better, or when it should be done, etc.

The most important principle in the opening is:

"Move every piece once before you move any piece twice, unless there is a tactic."

Every beginner should memorize this principle and try to follow it religiously (although advanced players know there are many exceptions).

By the way, applying this principle to the king means finding a good place to put it in the middlegame, which almost always involves castling. For these purposes, castling is considered developing the king, but not necessarily the castled rook, unless the castled square is already the correct developing square for that rook.

To show you how difficult this principle is for beginners to follow, I have privately tutored perhaps 700 players who were weak enough that they clearly were not following this principle. How did I know? I could see them moving the same pieces over and over in their games while some of their army remained dormant. So I had this discussion with them about sports teams using the maximum number of players, and showed them high-level games where good players utilized all their forces efficiently.

After this talk, how many of those 700 were immediately able to start following this important principle *(Move every piece once before you move any piece twice, unless there is a tactic)* consistently once they heard it and were aware of how important I thought it was for them?

The answer is one. That's right, just one. It was quite a few years ago, and he was a young professor at Temple University. I had this discussion and from then on he tried to do it the best he could in every game. I was amazed, since no one had been able to do it before, even though I thought it really wasn't all that difficult. And in all the years since, there has not been one more.

Once I had an adult student at my home who heard this and banged on the table (he was a big guy!), *"I will be the second!"* However, in the very next lesson he showed me a game he had recently played and sure enough, he had moved a piece twice unnecessarily. *"Oh well,"* I exclaimed, *"One for 301"* (as the count of students who had failed was at the time).

Don't get me wrong. Many of those students *eventually* realized that moving the same pieces multiple times, especially to make easily defended threats, was not such a good idea. And those who stopped playing like beginners of course eventually became much stronger players.

A good corollary of *"Use all your pieces all the time"* is:

"Taking a piece that is doing nothing and moving it to do something is likely more helpful than taking a piece that is doing something and trying to make it do more."

This is similar to the more well-known principle:

"Find your worst piece and make it better."

I think one of the reasons it is so difficult for beginners to follow the principle of, *"Move every piece once before you move any piece twice, unless there is a tactic"* is that other beginners often fall for cheap, easily defended threats. This makes making those "bad" threats psychologically desirable, because they often get their intended results due to the opponent's bad play. But pieces that are already in play are much more likely to be able to make these unwise threats than pieces stuck on the first rank, so moving them again is very tempting.

However, once you start playing against players who see your easy threats and consistently guard against them, the psychological temptation to make such threats gets quickly diminished. Here's a well-known example I use:

	White	**Black**
1.	e4	e5
2.	♘f3	♘c6
3.	♗c4	♗c5
4.	0-0	♘f6

White to move after 4...♘f6
Black

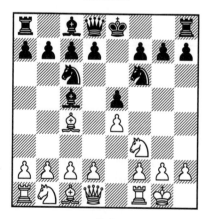

White

Suppose White now plays the tempting **5.♘g5?**. There are two threats: 6.♘xf7 forking the queen and rook, and 6.♗xf7+. But Black has a simple and strong defense:

Black to move after 5.♘g5
Black

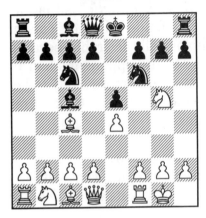

White

Black can just play **5...0-0** and White's 5.♘g5 looks silly since the knight on g5 is actually placed worse than it was on f3, and Black wanted to castle anyway. Beginners make these types of easily met threats all the time. And here, as advertised, White unwisely moved his king's knight a second time instead of doing something constructive like 6.♘c3 or 6.d3 (opening up the c1-h6 diagonal so he could develop his other bishop).

> ## Use all your pieces all the time.

Summary

Believe it or not, if you just do these three things well:

- Make safe moves and take advantage when your opponent makes unsafe ones (and I don't mean computer-difficult safety issues, but just mundane ones of a few ply);

- Move at just the right speed intending to use almost all your time, and allocate more time to the moves that need it; and

- Use all your pieces all the time

...then you can beat many, if not most, of the tournament players in the world, even if the rest of your strategy is not all that wonderful or you have not memorized a book on the Caro-Kann. You won't be an expert or a master, but you will have made some wonderful first steps.

Chapter 11

"Don't Stop Now!": Quiescence Errors

There is a type of error in chess which is very prevalent and, in a large measure, helps to separate the men from the boys. In *Chess Psychology*, GM Krogius gives this thought-process mistake the name *quiescence error,* meaning that a player erroneously stops analyzing, thinking the position is quiet when it is not.

What does "quiet" mean in this context? It means there are no more forcing moves (checks, captures, or threats) that are meaningful enough to possibly merit further investigation. So the position is able to be evaluated (Who stands better? How much better? Why are they better?).

When you analyze, you try to reach quiescent positions so you can evaluate them. As a silly counter-example, you would not analyze capturing your opponent's queen with your queen and evaluate yourself as ahead a queen if the opponent can just recapture your queen. The position after your initial capture is not quiescent – the opponent can recapture and regain the material, so you have to analyze at least that far before you might be able to evaluate.

Another simple example of a quiescence error should suffice:

(see diagram next page)

White to move
Black

White

Except for beginners, most players should recognize that White is not just losing his queen for a rook if he plays 1.♕e8+ ♖xe8 because White can then recapture 2.♖xe8 mate. To stop after 1...♖xe8 and think that White is losing material would be a quiescence error, albeit a simple one. White has a further check, 2.♖xe8 mate, which is not only check, but a forced mate.

In that sense White is not really sacrificing his queen because there is no risk. Some call 1.♕e8+ a "sham sacrifice" and others call it a "pseudo-sacrifice" but, no matter the name, White is just checkmating by force.

Very few experienced players would make a quiescence error in this position and not play 1.♕e8+. However, in actual play the quiescence error is one of the bigger differences between stronger and weaker players. Weaker players see sacrifices and think, "I can't do that. I am losing material." Stronger players think instead, "If I play that and give up material, are there further forcing moves I should investigate that might be worthwhile and make this sacrifice worth considering with additional analysis?

If the answer is No, then the strong players also drop the line as just losing material. But if the answer is Yes, then they analyze further to see if the initial sacrifice might be justified, or even clearly winning.

This is also the reason why many weaker players get these pseudo-sacrifices correct in a tactics book, but consistently miss them in a game. In the book, they know there is a solution, so that "overcomes" the quiescence error and forces them to look further until they find the solution. However, in a game, they don't know that there must be a payoff so, instead of possibly investigating further as they should, they just eliminate the line and miss that the sacrifice is good. I know this is so because I either have them think out loud or, when a student shows me a game where they miss such an "easy" sacrifice, I ask them why they missed it and the answer usually boils down to a quiescence error ("I did not see that it was actually good...").

Let's look at a game! I call this "The Immortal Quiescence Error Game" because in the middle of the game (moves 31-35) my student, playing White, made five (!) consecutive quiescence errors, some similar, some different. It's easy to miss the same idea multiple times once you miss it the first time, but here each was at least slightly different. I will not provide extensive notes about the remainder of the game, but it's pretty interesting.

White (1540) – Black (1549)
Sicilian Defense, Moscow Variation [B52]
Internet Chess Club, March 2013
G/45 with a 45-second increment

1.	e4	c5
2.	♘f3	d6
3.	♗b5+	♗d7
4.	♗xd7+	♛xd7
5.	0-0	♘f6
6.	♖e1	e5
7.	d3	♗e7
8.	♘c3	♘c6

9. ♗g5	0-0
10. ♗xf6	♗xf6

Black is playing so quickly that he has about 53½ minutes on his clock, up from the initial 45! When your opponent plays that quickly, think *"Thanks for the handicap!"* and keep playing at the normal (slower) speed! Don't make the beginner mistake of playing fast *"just because my opponent was playing fast, too."*

11. ♘d5	♗d8
12. c3	♛e6
13. ♛c2	f5
14. ♛b3	♛f7
15. c4?	

Up to here both sides have played reasonably with a small White advantage, but White should have played a move like 15.♖e2, guarding f2. Now Black has 15...fxe4! 16.dxe4 ♘d4! with a nice advantage, but instead he plays...

15...	f4

Nevertheless, Black still has some kingside initiative by pushing his pawns, which he does.

16. ♛d1	g5
17. ♘d2	h5
18. h3	♛g6
19. f3	

The engine likes 19.g4! with a small advantage for Black.

19...	♔f7

Better is 19...♖f7 with a large advantage.

20. ♔h1	♖h8

20...g4! is better. Now White can play 21.♖g1 with only a small edge for Black. However, for some strange reason Black keeps delaying the obvious, and good, idea of ...g5-g4 opening up the white king.

21. ♔g1	♕h6

Black still has over 52 minutes remaining, but finally begins to slow down as the game gets more complicated.

22. ♖b1	♗a5
23. ♖f1	♔e6
24. ♘b3	♖ag8?

24...♗b6 is at least equal.

25. ♘xa5	♘xa5
26. ♕a4	

White is properly counterattacking on the queenside. Even better is 26.b4!.

26...	♘c6
27. b4	♕h7?

Better is 27...♕g7! with attacking chances. Now White starts to seize his chance.

28. bxc5!	dxc5
29. ♕b5	♖g7
30. ♕xc5	g4?!

Better is 30...♖c8, but Black is losing anyway. Instead, he understandably finally tries to break through to the white king and the fun begins...

White to move
Black

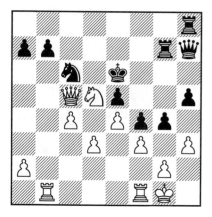

White

31. h4?

White thinks he is losing a rook after 31.♖xb7! ♖xb7, but that is just a quiescence error. It doesn't take much time to look one move further and find 32.♕xc6+ ♔f7 33.♕xb7+ and White is winning easily. He could also play another pseudo-sacrifice 31.♘xf4+ exf4 32.♕d5+ ♔f6 33.♕d6+ ♔g5 ("better" but dead lost is 33... ♔f7 34.♖xb7+) 34.♖b5+ ♔h4, and now 35.♕xf4 or 35.♕f6+ with mate to follow. This idea of taking on f4 to clear the d5 square for a deadly queen check remains for several moves, but with different consequences.

31...   **gxf3**

(see diagram next page)

White to move
Black

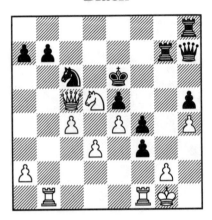

White

32. ☐xf3?

This time White misses 32.♘xf4+ exf4 33.♕d5+ ♔f6 (33...♔e7 34.☐xb7+ wins) 34.♕d6+ ♔f7 35.☐xb7+ ♔g8 36.♕e6+ ☐f7 37.♕e8+ ☐f8 38.♕xc6 with a crushing attack.

Note also that 32.☐xb7??, the same idea that was winning on the previous move, is not good any more, as Black does not have to play the obliging 32...☐xb7?? 33.♕xc6+ but instead wins with 32...☐xg2+ 33.♔h1 ♕xb7 guarding the c6-knight. Note that the changes since the previous move make all the difference; that often happens in complicated positions.

White thought that after 32.♘xf4+ exf4 he was just losing a knight, and did not bother to ask whether further analysis might show that line to be fruitful. Of course, the clearance of the square d5 by the initial knight check allows White to continue the attack with 33.♕d5+ and, once you realize that and analyze further, you might start to see that White gets his material back and more.

Again, you don't have to see past about the third move to realize White is chasing Black all over the board with continued threats. *You don't need to see the line to the end to realize it's really good for White.*

32...	♖hg8

White to move
Black

White

33. ♖f2?

This time White's forcing sequence to win is 33.♘xf4+ exf4 34.♕d5+ ♚f6 35.♖xf4+.

33...	♖g4

White to move
Black

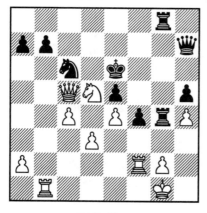

White

34. 罝fb2?

White has 34.♘xf4+ exf4 35.♕d5+ ♔f6 36.♕d6+ ♔g7 37.罝xb7+ ♔h8 38.罝xh7+ ♔xh7 39.♕xc6+−.

34...   **罝b8**

White to move
Black

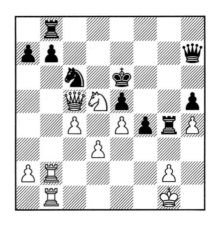

White

35. ♘b4?

The fifth straight quiescence error. Now it's back to the original idea of 35.罝xb7!, removing the guard on the c6-knight, and if 35...♕xb7 (also hopeless is 35...罝xb7 36.♕xc6+ +−) 36.罝xb7 罝xb7 37.♕xc6+ ♔f7 38.♕xb7+ wins easily. A fairly easy series of forcing captures.

35.♘xf4+ 罝xf4 36.♕d5+ is also good again.

Although none of the missed quiescence errors was trivial, all were straightforward enough that a strong class player (1600-2000) should be able to find each one most of the time in a slow game.

35...   **♘xb4**

Finally the game settles down – a little.

36. ♖xb4   ♛d7
37. ♛d5+?

Trading queens when your opponent's king is exposed and you are not way ahead in material is a definite no-no! White could play 37.♛xa7 with a big attack.

37...   ♛xd5
38. cxd5+   ♚d6
39. ♖xb7   ♖xb7
40. ♖xb7

White may be winning this endgame even if Black plays his best move, 40...♖g3, with the reply 41.♖h7.

40...   f3
41. ♖b2

Best but not so easy to spot is the interesting move 41.g3!.

41....   fxg2
42. ♖xg2   ♖xh4
43. ♖g6+   ♚d7
44. ♖g7+   ♚d6
45. ♖xa7   ♖h3
46. ♖a6+   ♚d7
47. ♖h6

Saving the pawn with 47.♖a3 is best and probably winning.

47...   ♖xd3
48. ♖xh5   ♚d6
49. ♖h6+

49.♚f2 is best, e.g. 49...♖d2+ 50.♚e3 ♖xa2 51.♖h6+ ♚d7 52.♖e6 and White will reach a winning position after capturing on e5 (as verified by a chess "tablebase," which solves chess for six or fewer pieces).

49...   ♔d7

49...♔c5! is better and should draw.

50. ♖e6	♖d1+
51. ♔f2	♖d2+
52. ♔e3	♖xa2
53. ♖xe5	♖a3+
54. ♔f4	♖a1
55. ♖f5	♖f1+
56. ♔e5	♖e1
57. ♖f7+	♔e8
58. ♖a7	♖e2
59. d6	♖h2

White to move
Black

White

60. d7+??

Pushing the pawn "past its zone of protection" and also setting up possible stalemate defenses. In general, in a rook-and-connected-passed-pawn endgame you would want to keep the pawns in communication with one another (in a king-and-pawn endgame, often the opposite is easiest). White had many winning moves instead, e.g. 60.♔d5 or 60.♔e6 or even "nothing" moves like 60.♖c7, waiting to make progress next move.

60...	**♔d8**
61. ♔d4	**♖d2+**
62. ♔e5	**♖h2!**

Avoiding the disastrous 62...♖xd7?? 63.♖xd7 ♔xd7 64.♔f6, when White wins.

63. ♔f5	**♖h5+**
64. ♔g6	**♖e5**
65. ♖a4	**♔xd7**
66. ♖d4+	**♔e6**
67. ♖a4	**♖b5**
68. ♖a1	**♔e5**
69. ♖e1	

Game drawn by mutual agreement. ½-½

So there was more to learn in this game than just the quiescence errors. However, keep in mind that if you see a candidate move that might lose material, ask, *"If I play this move and my opponent captures the material, are there further forcing moves which might make further investigation worthwhile?"* If so, try to look a little deeper and see if you might come out ahead after all when the smoke clears.

Chapter 12

//

Make Your Study Fun

Unlike school subjects, where study is mandatory if you wish to pass, chess is a hobby. I assume that playing chess is fun or you would not be reading this book.

However, there are many aspects of chess other than just "playing" which are involved in becoming a good player. Even within the game, there are aspects that are likely more fun than others.

For example, suppose you are playing in a tournament with a long time control and you have sufficient time on the clock. Suppose further that you have reached a complicated position where long and careful analysis would be required to attempt to find the best move. Would you find taking those 15-20 minutes of painstaking analysis fun?

In a quick survey of my Main Line Chess Club several years ago, many admitted that such work would not be fun and, moreover, when such situations arise, they just don't do it. After all, chess has to be fun for them and if an aspect is not fun, they are much less likely to spend the effort.

Yet if you ask strong players if taking those 15-20 minutes to carefully analyze is fun, almost all of them (including me) will reply, "Yes!" (or at least the older ones would when they were younger, but that's a different story!).

This capability to have fun while doing the most intense work is key to getting expertise at many different vocations and avocations, and not just chess. Let's list some other chess "work" that many might shun while others find enjoyable:

Make Your Study Fun

When I first started studying chess, I found the extremely helpful annotated game books to be fun to read. I read about 2,000 annotated games in my first 3-4 years of play. Even though I did not "memorize" any of the games, reading that many games gave me, almost by osmosis, a feel for how to play almost any position. In some senses, I could not put the books down; each game was like reading a mini-Sherlock Holmes mystery:

- *"How did Capablanca get such a good position without any tactics, and how was he going to finish off his opponent from this good position?"*
- *"How was Alekhine able to tie down his opponent in one half of the board, and then swiftly switch the attack to decisively win on the other side?"*
- *"How did Botvinnik learn the secret of that opening so that he was able to improve and get such a promising position so soon?"*
- *"Why did Fischer play such a dangerous move? Was it possible to calculate that his queen would not get trapped with so many delicate lines?"*

Yet, when I give an assignment to read similar games to my students, many find it not nearly as much fun, or not fun at all.

One of the reasons some find it not fun is that for some reason, without asking, they assume they have to read every sideline written by the author. And some also assume that to really learn from the game, they have to read it multiple times (as suggested by some instructors).

Yet when I read those books, I rarely played out elaborate sidelines. I estimate that in those 2,000 games I only played out about 15% of the sidelines and almost never played a game over more than once.

When my students hear that, they are relieved, but I almost always get the same response:

Chapter 12

"But if you don't play out all the sidelines, won't you learn less?"

The surprising answer is *"No!"*, but it takes some explaining:

Of course you will learn less *per unit game* if you only play it out once and skip some of the sidelines. However, the more times you review the same game, the less you will get out of each further review, because of diminishing returns on the information you did not get on the previous passes.

So if you review two games and get 50% of what you need to learn out of each game, it is almost always better than if you review the same game twice and get 50% on the first pass and then 50% of that (50% x 50%) = 25% on the second pass.

Now if there were a small, finite number of games you could review, getting 75% out of each game in twice the time might be better than getting 50% out of two games each in half the time. However, the supply of games is so large (and growing weekly) that no one can ever read every good annotated game. So it's much better to read more games with slightly less efficiency than it is to read far fewer games and get more out of each game.

So the key is that with such a large number of games available, you don't want to maximize your learning per unit game, you want to maximize your learning *per unit time*. So I can learn more in 100 hours going over many more games and, as a bonus, reading more different authors to get various points of view and reach some consensus on these viewpoints.

To add an exclamation point, for me it is *much* more fun to read a game the first time than to read it the second time. After all, it's like a book – after the first time I know the ending and how it all comes out. So reading all "first times" is much more enjoyable.

But what about those sidelines?

Same idea: *Maximize your learning per unit time.*

So if you skip the sidelines that don't look fun and only do the work that is fun, you are learning more because you are having more fun – and less likely to put down the book. Moreover, you are not just skipping those lines and replacing them with nothing; you are instead reading more games in that time because it takes you less time to go over each game if you don't have to play out each sideline. The result is that in the same amount of time it would have taken you to play out some games and all the sidelines you can read more games and have more fun. So there's no great reason to force yourself to read all the sidelines.

> You want to maximize your learning per unit time, not per unit game studied.

Did I ever read the sidelines? Of course! Sometimes I am attracted to read the sideline because it is short and easy, sometimes because I am very curious as to what would have happened on those "obvious" alternative moves, and sometimes because I see further text in the sideline that makes a point that seems important (and thus I want to see what all the fuss is about by playing the sideline at least up to that position where the text occurs).

Whenever a student says that homework is not fun, I give them one of my cardinal rules:

Never, ever do homework that's not fun!

If you do persist on plowing through chess work that's not fun, you will learn less and probably resent me (or whomever) more for assigning it. Moreover, almost no one can keep up doing homework that's not fun very long, at least not in a hobby.

Once in a while, I get a student who says, *"I will do the homework even though it's not fun because I want to be a good player, and if this is what I have to do to become a good player, then I will force myself to do it!"*

That never works for very long! If an aspect of a hobby is not fun, then that aspect will either ruin your hobby or you will eventually learn to skip it.

So what if certain homework is not fun and you should not do it? What should you do?

If you are my student, the next step is to tell me that the work is not fun and I will ask you why. Sometimes it's not fun because you are either misunderstanding the assignment or doing it wrong. The example above where students hate playing out games because going through all the sidelines is such drudgery. That's easily solved.

Of course, sometimes the homework can't be made fun. One reason why some players get much better than others is not because they are more intelligent or have more time, but because for them all the work is fun. They like spending time on complicated moves in long games. They can't wait to see how Spassky won that next game and what Author So-and-so will say about it. They love chess puzzles of all types, even the types that are not "Play and win" such as helpmates or Jeff Coakley's challenging Switcheroos.

Switcheroo: Switch *any* two pieces on the board and leave Black in a legal checkmate.

To be legal, you can't switch pawns to the first or eighth ranks and the position must be able to occur in a real game. You can switch pieces of any color.

Switcheroo Problem
Black

White

Answer: Only switching the queen on e4 with the pawn on b3 works.

Switching the black pawn on f7 with the white queen (or other pieces) may be checkmate, but it's impossible to reach positions with those double checks in a real game. This type of problem may also be considered a "board vision" problem because, although you can't switch pieces in a real game, it tests and extends your skill at visualizing solutions while enhancing your ability to construct legal checkmates. Of course, the main idea is that it is not only instructive, but for most good players this type of puzzle is fun, and that's the purpose of this chapter!

Getting back to our discussion on "all is fun" players, they make time to go to many tournaments. After their games, win or lose, they enjoy reviewing those games with their opponents and stronger players and seek out constructive criticisms. It's all fun for them.

But some chessplayers, even those dying to get better, find some of the work just that – hard work. And no matter how we slice it and dice it, we can't make that aspect fun. Does that mean they should give up chess? Of course not. I'll bet even some grandmasters found certain aspects (but not too many!) of their work less fun, but were able to work around it, so to speak.

For things like spending time on critical positions in slow games, there is no workaround. But for others, like reviewing annotated games, maybe the student is lucky enough to enjoy game videos instead. Then the challenging thing is to find videos that are just the right level for the kind of improvement information they need. That isn't easy. It's relatively easy to tell a 1500 player that he will learn a lot more from my *The World's Most Instructive Amateur Game Book* or Chernev's *The Most Instructive Games Ever Played* than from *Karpov's Best Games* or Kasparov's *The Test of Time* (those latter two excellent books are not primarily meant for instruction). But it's not nearly so easy (to put it mildly!) to know which of the millions of videos online and on DVD are just right for a particular student.

What are some other things you can do to make chess study fun?

- If a puzzle is not fun because it is timed, then don't time it or ignore the timing and just learn from the puzzle at your leisure. If the puzzle is not fun because it is *not* timed, then see how fast you can do it correctly or how many you can do in a certain amount of time.

- Take statistics. See if you can do a puzzle set faster or more accurately than you did before. Find out which openings give you the highest performance rating.

- Speed games help all kinds of chess improvement, from openings to tactical awareness to time management. But if you don't like speed games, then don't play them, as you will get diminishing returns on types of play you don't find fun. On the other hand, if you like speed games, you may find them more fun (and much more helpful) if you use the same kind of increment that you encounter in serious slow games, to train your brain for how to think in time trouble when it really means something.

- Get a *study buddy,* a friend close to your playing strength who would like to study with you. Learning an opening is a lot more fun if you can play one side and someone else plays the other (plus you can discuss why those moves are made as opposed to other possibilities). Or you can play speed games with those openings and look them up after each set of games. Or you can review your (or your study-buddy's) games together and talk about what you are learning. You can even do that with annotated game books. You can play out interesting or "technique" positions against your study-buddy to see what you can learn. Assuming your study-buddy is near your playing strength, learn from your study-buddy what he is good at that you are not, and return the favor by helping him in the aspects of the game in which you are superior.

- Organize events you like, either live or online via servers like the Internet Chess Club or Chess.com. For example, to promote slow chess on Chess.com, David G and I started the Dan Heisman Learning Center. When I would show up at a chess club and they were not holding events that I thought fun, I offered to organize such events. Maybe your local coffee house would love to host a chess night, once per week, where events you find fun can be the main focus. Use your imagination, but be proactive!

Chapter 13

Chess Etiquette

According to legend, a chess journalist once asked Bobby Fischer – who was famous not only for being a great chessplayer but also for being "difficult" – if he liked to bother his opponents.

"*Yes!*", Fischer immediately answered.

Sensing a juicy reply, the questioner quickly followed up, "*And what do you do?!*"

"*Oh, I make good moves!*"

Not many of us can make good moves like Bobby Fischer, but everyone should know about chess etiquette. Sometimes it is hard to find this information, but sooner or later most tournament players figure it out – sometimes the hard way.

> How did Fischer like to purposely upset his opponents? By making good moves!

Some chess etiquette is so important that it is written into the official rules. If that is the case, then we will mark that advice with an extra (R) below to denote "Rule."

All the Time vs. Formal Play

We can separate etiquette into two types:

- etiquette that applies all the time, whether in a friendly game or a serious one; and
- etiquette that is more particular to tournament play.

In a tournament, if you have any question about the rules, including enforcing etiquette, you may stop the clock (if you are using one and it is your turn), and ask the Tournament Director (TD). The U.S. Chess Federation (USCF) certifies TD's, who are not representatives of the USCF, but must enforce/follow the USCF rules or they may lose their USCF license to run rated tournaments.

All the Time

The following etiquette rules apply all the time...

Don't Bother Your Opponent in Any Way

This rule (R) takes many forms, from asking questions (even when it is your move – your opponent also has the right to think on your time!), making noises, talking loudly or unnecessarily with others, moving the table or pieces, making distracting motions, displacing the clock, **Talking is a no-no** obstructing the board – anything your opponent legitimately finds distracting (and most U.S. tournaments are now "No Smoking"). The list could go on for an entire book! But most importantly, I should repeat, chess is a quiet game!

Chess should be played without talking (the exceptions are draw offers, indicating the stopping of a clock – on your time – to get the TD, adjusting pieces on your time, indicating a rules violation such as touch move, and emergencies. (Calling "check" is optional – see the paragraph below on Calling Check). Of course, if your opponent finds your quiet breathing distracting, he should purchase a good noise protection device and not pester the TD to stop you from breathing...

Greet Your Opponent

Always greet your opponent at the start of a game. A handshake and a friendly *"Hi, my name is____"* is a good minimum. Most players, at the start of a tournament game with an unfamiliar opponent, check the player's name (and rating!) to see if they are facing the correct player, and make a little small talk such as asking how the opponent is doing, where are they from, and even wishing them "Good luck" (even if they don't really mean it), etc. Usually a handshake (or sometimes a second one if it has been a while since you both first sat down) precedes the starting of the clock. Black is expected to start the clock so that White can move, but if Black is not present White may move immediately and start the clock (R).

When and How to Resign

The president of my first chess club gave me the following advice, which I will paraphrase:

"Dan, you are a beginner. Our club has many fine players who will be willing to play you. When you play them, you have two choices if you are losing to a much better player. If you reach a position where you could beat them easily, the proper thing is to resign and thereby not insult them as to their ability to checkmate you nor waste their time. However, if you are curious as to how they can best checkmate you, you may play the game out to checkmate, but it is considered bad manners to make them play all that extra time and then resign right before checkmate, so let them mate you."

I should hasten to add that if you are facing a player considerably worse than you are, you should be hesitant about resigning too soon. If you are playing an absolute beginner, he may have no idea at all how to checkmate you from a superior position and many will stalemate you or draw through the fifty-move rule or even with a king and queen (or more) vs. your lone king, so I wouldn't resign against beginners at all.

By the way, there are several ways to resign. You can say "I resign," or "I give up;" you can purposely lay down your king. Many players just reach out to unilaterally stop their clock and offer a handshake, although this can be a little tricky (see Chapter 5, "Know the Rules").

A word of warning, however: handshakes do not end the game. If someone offers you a draw (see offering a draw below), you may say "I accept" and offer your hand as a signal of acceptance. To decline, simply say "I decline," "No," make a move, or say "let me think about it," after which you may do any of the others. (R)

A young student of mine did not know that shaking hands could be misinterpreted as ending the game (see Chapter 5). Therefore, since he was brought up to always shake an offered hand, he did so! This ended up causing a problem although eventually the game did continue, but the lesson is clear: "Don't shake hands unless you agree that the game is over!"

Way of Moving Pieces

Some players like to intimidate their opponents by banging down their pieces to emphasize a good move. Others like to screw the pieces into the board. Any similar behavior is viewed unfavorably by the majority of chessplayers. If you have an opponent who consistently does these things to an annoying degree, you may ask the TD to request that your opponent stop doing so.

Answering a Request to Play a Game

Recently I was at my local chess club there were only three strong players present – two others and myself. The other two were playing a short game. I asked if I could play the winner. The players vaguely nodded their assent and I awaited the finish by walking around the club. When I came back, the game was over, but the players were analyzing the position. I helped them analyze for a while, but they wanted to continue to analyze, so I again strolled around because I didn't want to interfere too much.

A few minutes later I came back and they had started another game! I considered this quite rude, as it was obvious that the players had waited for me to walk away so they could continue to play each other. If they *did not* want me to play the winner, it would have been correct etiquette for them to simply answer my request, *"No thanks, we just want to play each other this evening."* I would not have been upset if they had done this. If they *did* want me to play, I was only within 20 feet of their game, so it would have taken very little effort to locate me. But *not* clearly turning down my request combined with *not* letting me play (I could have played a weaker player instead of waiting) was clearly a breach of etiquette.

There is also the question of game conditions. In a tournament these are clearer, but informally there is the question of using a clock (some beginners are vehemently opposed) and, if so, how long the game should be. Normally these things are easily worked out. However, if you are playing without a clock and your opponent is taking too long, welcome to the club! Maybe next time you will want to play with a clock, too. As to the other conditions, normally chess is played with a Staunton design set (R), and if there is more than one game the players will alternate colors. If you play White first and win quickly (so that there is still plenty of time for more games), it is especially considerate to offer to let the other player have White, too, and not just seek a stronger opponent.

Formal Play

The following types of etiquette primarily are used in formal (tournament, match) play.

When to Stop the Clock

There are only two correct times (R) to stop the clock: 1) When the game is over, and 2) When one of the players is on the move and he wishes to ask the TD a question about the rules or make a claim. If you have to go to the bathroom, just make your move, push the clock  as normal, and go to the bathroom. It is also considered incorrect (R) to otherwise touch the clock during play. For example, you should not rest your non-moving hand on the clock, nor should you pull the clock in front of you to read the time remaining. Occasionally, players are allowed to angle the clock momentarily toward them to better read the time remaining, but they should not do so if their opponent is about to hit the clock, and they must return the clock to a position that is equally accessible to both players.

By the way, people who have never played with a clock before often forget to hit the clock after their turn. It is polite to remind them a few times early in the game, at least often enough so that they should get the idea. However, there is no requirement for you to help your opponent and, if he forgets to hit his clock during time pressure, you do not have to let him know. Just think normally; if your time is short and you are not moving quickly, most opponents will look at the clock and realize they forgot to hit it. If they get upset, they should be upset with themselves for not hitting the clock, and not with you for not telling them. After all, it is their responsibility to hit the clock, not yours to tell them if they didn't.

In one of the crucial Kasparov-Karpov World Championship matches, Kasparov was in time trouble and did not push the clock after making his move. Karpov correctly did not tell him and, when a minute later Kasparov realized his error, he was upset. However, it seemed to me that Kasparov was upset with himself for making such an elementary error, and not at his longtime foe for not telling him.

Offering and Accepting a Draw

There is only one acceptable time to offer a draw (R): after you move, but before you push the clock. Since there is a responsibility to move, if your opponent offers a draw while he is thinking, you should politely ask him, *"please make your move and I will consider it."* Because he made an illegal offer, he is not allowed to withdraw his offer, even if he finds a move that convinces him that he is winning, nor may he threaten to withdraw his offer if you don't take it immediately.

Once, not soon after I started playing tournaments, I offered a draw during my move to a master who I had beaten previously. The above rule was not in effect in those days, so the master, who was looking for revenge, immediately said no. I then found a winning continuation and played the winning move. The master thought for a while, smiled, and humorously asked, *"You still don't want that draw, do you?"* I smiled, said no, and won. Under today's rules, he would have asked me to make the move, waited to see how good it was, and then wisely accepted!

Calling Check

Although many years ago (even before I was born!), the rules required you to say "check," those days are long gone. USCF rules (R) *allow* you to call check, but don't *require* it. I teach all my students not to say check. My reasoning is as follows: in tournament play, where all the players are experienced, it is considered somewhat to very insulting to call check – it is as if you are implying

You don't have to call check

your opponent is a beginner who cannot see for himself that he is in check. Therefore, almost no good player calls check. But where does one draw the line? Do you call check to players rated Under 1000 but not above? No matter how you do it, it eventually always causes a problem. Secondly, calling check to a low-rated player is helping him. You wouldn't tell him that you are threatening to fork his queen and rook with a knight. If he doesn't see that he is in check and touches another piece, which then has to be used to get out of check, then you are helping him learn to look to see what his opponent's moves are doing. A player who loses because he didn't see he was in check did so because of his lack of knowledge, board vision, discipline, or whatever. In any case, each player should learn to carefully look to see what his opponent's move did, whether or not it was a check.

Calling checkmate has similar problems. Take, for example, two of my young students who were playing each other in a tournament. One of the players (who was otherwise losing) thought he had a checkmate and stood up and cried, *"Checkmate!"* The other player, younger by a couple of years, felt the pressure and thus could not find either of his two legal replies, the best of which would leave him up two pieces. They asked me if it was checkmate, but I replied that I was not allowed to help them during a tournament game – I could cite the rule for checkmate, but not tell them if a position was checkmate until the game was over. Finally the younger one agreed that he was check-mated and stopped the clock. At that point I said that I was allowed to comment and tried to politely show them that the move wasn't checkmate. The result? The younger player began to cry.

I told his friend that it was a good example of why you shouldn't call checkmate – I don't teach my students to try to intimidate their opponents into resigning, so little good can happen by exclaiming checkmate. If it is checkmate, you should just push the clock as normal and let your opponent tell you that he is mated; if it isn't checkmate, you will probably save yourself the embarrassment of calling checkmate when it is not.

Using *J'Adoube*

When a piece accidentally gets put somewhere other than the middle of a square, you may adjust it (R) by first saying "*J'adoube*" (French for "I adjust") or "adjust." You may only do so on your move, no matter whose piece it is, and you must say so before adjusting. If you accidentally knock over a piece on the way to move another piece, as soon as you finish moving, you should say "*J'adoube*" and adjust the piece *before you hit the clock*. Similarly, if the piece you just moved falls over, you should adjust it before you hit the clock, if you can do so.

Enforcing Rules

Except for cheating that is observed where an opponent would not be able to detect it, no third party may interfere with a game (R). Therefore, besides the TD in certain situations, the only one who can enforce rules broken by your opponent is you. You have the option to call touch move, or point out any illegal moves (sometimes if it is in your favor to not enforce a rule, you do not have to do so).

As in golf, to enforce rules is not a breach of etiquette; quite the contrary, it is expected that each player will enforce the rules and when you do so, assuming you do it politely and correctly, no opponent should be upset or ask you to excuse him.

Moreover, you should not decide which parts of the rule book you should enforce. You should not let your opponent get away with touch move, but call an illegal move if he jumps his bishops over pawns. You put yourself in an awkward position if you decide that you will enforce some rules but not others. Big arguments have started over players feeling that their opponents let them get away with something but not something else. A rule is a rule.

Here is one exception: suppose you are playing a beginner who makes many illegal moves. You probably should get the tournament director the first time to explain the illegality and possibly enforce the appropriate penalty. However, after that, if you are winning easily (as you should!) and further illegal moves are not having an effect on your winning chances, then you can politely refrain from calling the TD. Instead just gently inform the beginner that his move was illegal and allow him to retract it and find a legal one on his own time.

Third-Party Interference/Observing Other Games

At scholastic tournaments, I sometimes see uninformed spectators think they are doing the players a favor by pointing out that a move is illegal – for example, when one of the players does not move out of check. This is no favor! Such interference can have a strong effect on the outcome of the game, and is illegal. The best way to put it is: *Chess is a game between two players; besides the TD, no one else may interfere!* (R)

In the above example, the knowledge and skill of the players with regard to recognizing check and knowing what to do when there is a rules violation is part of the game. If a player loses because he does not recognize check or is unwilling to ask a TD for help, then that can work against him/her. At the start of every tournament I tell the players,

Chess Etiquette

"If you run into any situation for which you have a question, or if anything unusual happens in your game, please stop the clock and get the TD."

If they do not get the TD or cannot recognize a problem, it is not up to a spectator to help them out. And helpful parents can be just that – helpful; that is not fair to their child's opponent, even if the interference is not for their own child's benefit. Anything which interferes with the players (and TD's) normal enforcement of the rules creates a potential unfairness.

> If you run into any situation for which you have a question, or if anything unusual happens in your game, please stop the clock and get the TD.

Even the body language of the player's coaches or parents can have a strong effect on the game. I often see a player lift a piece for a move and then look at the coach/parent for approval. Since the touch-move rule only requires them to move the piece, and not to the square they are indicating, any frown or nod of approval is really just a form of cheating, however unintentional.

There is one exception to all the above. If an opponent is cheating away from the board (so that his opponent would have no way to tell), then any third party may intervene by informing the TD if they have enough proof. For example, if a player is overheard getting advice from a coach or observed using a computer, then a third party should notify the TD immediately.

By the way, a player is allowed to get up from their board and tell others how he is doing – but he may not get any feedback that could affect the game. As for generally talking to others while you are playing, I advise against it just because doing so may annoy your opponent and/or give the appearance of possibly soliciting advice.

Chapter 13

Summing Up

Most chess games are played without any etiquette problems. Experienced players know what to expect and try to do the same. Occasionally there is a disagreement among players with the best intentions, but if everyone uses good common sense (and the guidelines above), there are usually very few serious problems.

Chapter 14

//

Puzzles with a Point

A couple of years ago I was asked to write a column, "Puzzles with a Point," for Chess.com's *Master's Bulletin* magazine. I thought readers of this second edition would benefit from these instructive puzzles, so they are reprinted here with the permission of Chess.com.

While a couple of the Puzzles with a Point are somewhat more advanced than the material in the remainder of the book, most are quite in line with the spirit of *Everyone's Second Chess Book,* and thus all have been included.

Puzzle #1
What's an outside passed pawn?

Welcome to our new series, Puzzles with a Point.

In a sense, every chess puzzle has a point, but it's often a mundane one, such as:

- You should know this tactical pattern,
- See how beautifully the pieces work together, or
- Isn't this puzzle fiendishly difficult?

But this series attempts to provide puzzles that may do more than that, such as:

- Offer insight into common types of thought-process errors,
- Provide a key learning point, or
- Show some aspect of a stronger player's thought process

I got the idea for this first puzzle from backgammon books. Backgammon authors often use a helpful method for determining a plan. They show a position on the edge XY where if the position is better than the one given you do X and if it's worse you do Y. In chess, this would mean we give a position on the edge of a win/draw. If your position is better than the one given that barely wins, you are winning, while if it's slightly worse you are drawing".

Consider the following position:

Puzzle 1: White to move and win
Black

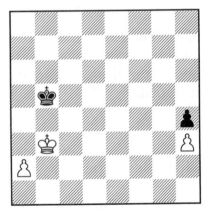

White

1.   ♔c3

In this position White has the extra passed a-pawn. I do not call White's a-pawn an outside passed pawn. I reserve the term "outside passed pawn" for the situation where *both* sides have passed pawns (say, add a black pawn on the c-file in this puzzle) and one player's pawn is further away from the side where the kings eventually have to race (here the h-file on the kingside). See our example diagram below.

(see diagram next page)

White to move (Outside passed pawn example)
Black

White

So in this second diagram, where Black *has* a c-pawn, White *does have the outside a-pawn* but, in our first diagram, the one that is our puzzle, White just has *the* passed pawn.

In the first diagram, White has two possible plans:

1. Bolt at once for the h-pawns, or
2. Push the a-pawn first.

Let's show that the latter plan is clearly worse (continuing from the diagram on page 170):

1.a3 ♔a5 2.♔c3 (or 2.a4 ♔b6 3.♔b4 ♔a6 4.a5 ♔b7 5.♔b5 ♔a7 6.a6 ♔b8 7.♔b6 ♔a8 8.♔c5 ♔a7 9.♔d5 ♔xa6 10.♔e5 ♔b6 11.♔f4 ♔c6 12.♔g4 ♔d6 13.♔xh4 ♔e7 14.♔g5 ♔f8 15.♔g6 ♔g8, draw) 2...♔a4 3.♔d4 ♔xa3 4.♔e4 ♔b4 5.♔f4 ♔c5 6.♔g4 ♔d6 7.♔xh4 ♔e7 8.♔g5 ♔f8 9.♔g6 ♔g8, draw.

So we can make a general conclusion: *when you have such an extra outside pawn, only push it as much as it takes to distract the enemy king to go get it.* In this case White does not have to distract the enemy king at all: Black is forced to get the pawn no matter where it is, so White should leave it alone. Pushing the pawn either doesn't help or, in this case, throws away the win

Returning to the first diagram after **1.♔c3,** play could continue **1...♚a4 2.♔d4 ♚a3 3.♔e4 ♚xa2 4.♔f4 ♚b3 5.♔g4 ♚c4 6.♔xh4 ♚d5 7.♔g5 ♚e6 8.♔g6 ♚e7 9.♔g7** and White wins by blocking the black king from getting to one of the critical squares f7 or f8.

Note that this is an "edge" position because if we make White's position any worse, the win turns into a draw, e.g.:

- Move the h-pawns back to h2 and h3 (try it!), or
- Start the white a-pawn at a3 or further up the board.

Of course, make White's initial position better and the win is even easier:

- Move the h-pawns to h4 and h5 or further up,
- Start the white king further toward the h-pawns, or
- Move the h-pawns to the g-file (non-rook pawns are much easier to promote, using the powerful principle, *"If the offensive king can get two or more ranks in front of a non-rook's pawn without trivially losing the pawn, then it's a win no matter where the defending king is nor does it matter whose move it is."*

So next time you have *the* passed pawn, be very careful before moving it! ☺

Puzzle #2
Don't automatically capture pinned pieces

(see diagram next page)

Puzzle 2: White to move
Black

White

Many years ago I wrote a "Novice Nook" column titled, "Examples of Chess Logic." It had to do with some common-sense ideas that you don't often read in chess texts. One of those ideas, which at first strikes some as absurd, is: *"Don't take off a pinned piece unless it is necessary for a tactic or offers some clear strategic advantage."*

Like all principles, it has exceptions, but it's a stronger principle than you might think. The basic idea is that pinned pieces, in general, can't move anyway until they are unpinned, so why not wait until the opponent uses a tempo to unpin them if you are going to eventually capture them? The following position is a good example where beginners would probably take the pinned piece without any thought at all (and I see them do so all the time in similar situations when I watch Internet games):

From the puzzle diagram, White should play 1.♘g3. For now, ignoring the trade of the bishop for the queen is the right idea. Black has to get out of the pin anyway, so he either has to capture the bishop himself or move the king first, losing a tempo. This valuable tempo can be used to attack the vulnerable h-pawn with **1.♘g3** (After 1.♗xg7+? ♔xg7, the black king is now one square closer to the h-pawn's defense: 2.♘g3 ♔g6 and White is ahead a pawn in a knight-and-pawn endgame with a tough road ahead to try and win.

I don't have access to a 7-piece tablebase, but it won't be easy.) **1...♔h7** (1...♕xc3 2.bxc3 is a similar endgame, except White has a c-pawn instead of a b-pawn, probably a minor help for Black but not significant [and the *Shredder* tablebase at http://www.shredderchess.com/online-chess/online-databases/endgame-database.html confirms this].) **2.♗xg7** (Now that Black has taken the tempo to remove the pin, other moves are weaker!) **2...♔xg7 3.♘xh5+.** The point of delaying the capture of the pinned piece; White has won an extra pawn and now the win is in sight. The tablebase says Black to play gets mated in 32 moves with perfect play on both sides.

White to move
Black

White

In the above diagram, only one thing has changed since our Puzzle 2 diagram, but it is a major change. Now Black has the big threat to save his queen by interposing with the knight next move, 1...♘d4 or 1...♘e5. This is a defensive tactic, saving material. Therefore, White does not have enough time to win the h-pawn and has to settle for 1.♗xg7+ ♔xg7 with "only" the better chances. Notice that this is *not* an exception to the principle, "Don't take off a pinned piece unless it is necessary for a tactic...," because Black was threatening a defensive tactic which could be executed if White did not make the capture **1.♗xg7+ ♔xg7.**

White to move
Black

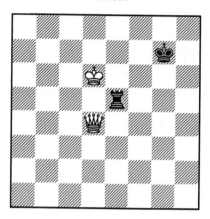

White

Our third diagram from Puzzle 2 is a trivial exception. White is winning easily and has no need to make Black lose a tempo (not that there are any tempos to be gained) and should just capture the pinned rook. It is mate in 5 with either recapture.

Summary: Pinned pieces, especially "absolutely pinned" pieces to the king, can't move anyway and aren't going anywhere. Therefore, unless there is a tactical reason to do otherwise (and there often is), it is usually correct to wait until the opponent spends a tempo to break the pin by moving the piece that it is pinned to, and then capture the pinned piece.

Puzzle #3
Asking the right questions

When Everyman Books asked me to select and update my best Novice Nooks into the book *A Guide to Chess Improvement*, they also asked me to write three new Novice Nooks that would never be published on the Web. I did that, and one of them was Section 2-8, *"Ask the Right Questions."* This article discusses how important it is, when analyzing, to realize what is going on and to be able to ask questions that will lead you to logical candidate moves and then to the eventual selection of one of the better ones. I cannot reproduce the article from that book, but I can provide a fresh approach on this important subject.

I first ran across the following problem in Irving Chernev's fun book *The Bright Side of Chess*. It was composed by Holst, and it is White to play and checkmate in three moves.

White to move and mate in 3
Black

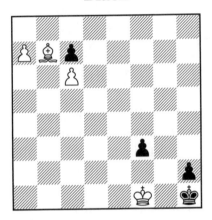

White

So the obvious question everyone would begin with is:

"How can White checkmate in three moves?"

However, after the "obvious" move 1.a8♕ and Black's forced reply 1...f2, a new question comes into play:

"How can White play a move like 2.♕g8, threatening mate, without stalemating Black?"

But this *"How does White avoid the stalemate?"* issue leads to the more straightforward question I used to solve the puzzle rather quickly. Do you know what that question was?

It was, *"Which Black piece is going to make the second move?"*

Now, to answer that question, let's start with another one.

"Suppose that Black's second move is made by the f-pawn. That means White is going to allow Black to promote. That further requires White to move his king off the f1 square. But is it possible the white king can go to a square where the f-pawn would not check upon promotion?"

Turns out that is not possible. For example, if 1.♔e1 f2+ 2.♔d2, Black can always play 2...f1♘+. So if the f-pawn is to make the second move for Black, it can always be check. The next question to ask is:

"Can White get out of check on the third move while simultaneously checkmating Black?"

In other words, can he allow the black pawn to promote, and capture it with mate? The answer is No; that would take a queen, and there is no way White can capture on f1 with a queen and simultaneously get the king out of the way to allow the black f-pawn to promote. That would take way too many moves.

We can also mention that 1.a8♕ f2 2.♔xf2 is stalemate, so that eliminates the possibilities with the f-pawn.

Therefore, Black's second move cannot be with the f-pawn! But if White is to keep the king on f1 and prevent the promotion with check, then the black king can't move either. And if the black king can't move, then neither can the pawn on h2. That means if there is going to be a solution to the problem, it must involve the pawn on c7 making the second move!

As Sherlock Holmes said, *"Once you eliminate the impossible, whatever remains, no matter how improbable, must be the truth."*

But the c7-pawn can only move by capturing on b6 or d6. So we should be able to restate the problem thus: *"White to play and put a piece on b6 or d6 on the second move."* But the bishop can't do that – wrong color – so it must be a promoting pawn. But a queen, rook, or bishop can't get from a8 to b6 or d6 in one move, so it must be a knight.

Therefore, the first move must be... **1.a8♘**, else we have proven there can't be any answer at all. Black's reply is forced:.. **1...f2.** White now has to give Black a second move and, as we have previously shown, 2.♔xf2 is stalemate and 2.♔e2 f1♕+ can't work, so... **2.♘b6 cxb6.** Forced. Now if White does not have a checkmate on the next move, then we have proven that no solution is possible, but... **3.c7 mate.**

By this questioning process, we have converted the original question, *"How can White checkmate in three moves?"* to, *"How can White give Black a second move without stalemating him?"* and finally to, *"Which black piece must make the second move?"*

Once we solved that, the rest was relatively easy. This is the type of "chess logic" you often use in tactical situations to find ways to win material, avoid losing material, checkmate, or avoid checkmate.

For example, rather than ask what a good move is, you might say, *"If I allow my opponent's queen to get up to h6 in the next two moves, would I be able to stop a subsequent checkmate, or must that not be allowed?"* or, *"Suppose the bishop retreats to the side of the board. If I move the knight that it can take, is it possible I can use my pawns to trap the bishop? If he can stop it, would the concessions he makes in his position to do so be enough to make it worthwhile to move the knight?"*

Strategic questions may include, *"What is my worst piece and how can I make it better?"* or, *"If I get X but have to weaken my pawn structure, what are the chances my opponent can take advantage of the pawn structure weaknesses and does that outweigh X?"*

Knowing which questions to ask – and having the ability to answer them quickly and relatively accurately – is one key skill in your arsenal of analysis weapons.

Puzzle #4
Don't jump to conclusions

When watching lower-rated players play king-and-pawn endgames, they often rush their king over to the opposition's pawns. And when I write "rush," I mean both in a tempo sense and in a time-clock sense. They do it quickly without much thought, as if this *has* to be the right idea.

In many cases rushing the king toward the pawns is, of course, correct, although taking time to see how best to go after the pawns is always a good idea. However, in some other positions, going straight toward the pawns is not such a good idea, and there are many puzzles which illustrate this.

White to move and win
Black

White

Puzzle #4 was composed by I. Dobias in 1926. In his original puzzle the white pawn was on f2, but it turns out f3 is just as good, and that was the way I remembered it, so I am showing it to you that way.

Chapter 14

The "natural" way for White to proceed is to go directly after the pawn at g6. Even if White is doing this without checking (a bad habit), he should at least take time to see if the path via e5 and f6 is superior to the path via f4 and g5. It turns out neither is sufficient to win: 1.♔e5 (1.♔f4 ♔c4 2.♔g5 ♔d4 3.♔xg6 *[3.f4 ♔e4=]* 3...♔e3=) 1...♔c4 2.♔f6 ♔d4 3.♔xg6 ♔e3=.

Once it is established that direct paths to the pawn don't win, it's time to investigate the main idea: first block the black king and then go after the pawn. To someone who has never seen a puzzle like this, the idea seems unlikely: why spend tempos with your king to make the other king spend tempos? But it turns out sometimes the tempos you spend are fewer than the tempos you cost your opponent, so the idea often has merit. The first move to try is to get "the opposition" with 1.♔d5.

1.♔d5. In this case the right idea for Black is to go "under" the white king and counterattack the white pawn and, indeed, this is still sufficient to draw: 1...♔b4 2.♔e6 (2.♔d4 ♔b3 3.♔d3 ♔b2 4.♔d2 ♔b3 5.♔e3 ♔c3 6.f4 ♔c4 7.♔e4 ♔c3 8.♔e5 ♔d3 9.♔f6 ♔e4=) 2...♔c4 3.♔f6 ♔d4 4.♔xg6 ♔e3=.

So if there is going to be a win, what can it be? The hint is that in the 1.♔d5 line the black king needed to go below the white king to counterattack the white pawn. Maybe if White anticipates that Black's king wants to get "under" his king and instead first tries... **1.♔d4! ♔b4 2.f4 ♔b3 3.♔e5 ♔c3 4.♔f6 ♔d4 5.♔xg6+−.** So that's it!

When you see even one problem like this, you should know next time you get into a king-and-pawn endgame that perhaps running right toward the enemy pawns may not be the best plan. It often is, but to do so without thought is always going to be a bad idea. Endgame prowess is not always memorizing a ton of endgame positions, but rather being aware of various possibilities and taking the time to calculate which ones work.

> King-and-pawn endgames are often very tricky and always critical. Take time to analyze carefully.

Puzzle #5
Extending your board vision

A while ago I wrote an article for Chess.com called, "Not 'White to Play and Win?' – Worthless?!" (http://www.chess.com/article/view/not-quotwhite-to-play-and-winquot-worthless).

The gist of that article is that a percentage of my students, and thus a percentage of the chess world in general, believe that puzzles that either alter the rules slightly or contain positions that cannot occur in games cannot be helpful. I make the analogy that using this logic would be like a football player claiming that lifting weights cannot be helpful because there are no weights on a football field!

The following puzzle is one of those "slightly altered" ones, a gem by Jeff Coakley, one of the great North American chess authors. His basic book *Winning Chess Strategy for Kids* is not just for kids, and is one of the best introductory strategy books I have seen. *Winning Chess Exercises for Kids* may be the best intermediate (yes, you read that correctly) puzzle book I've ever seen. Compare it to the classic Fred Reinfeld book *1,001 Chess Sacrifices and Combinations* (Coakley's book has 900) and Coakley's book is better in almost every conceivable respect.

Puzzle #5 is just one of many great board-vision puzzles presented in *Winning Chess Puzzles for Kids,* Vol. II (again, not just for kids...). Coakley calls this type of puzzle a "Double Whammy":

White to play and make two moves
in a row to checkmate Black
Black

White

The first move cannot be check. Black does not move, so it's not like a mate-in-two.

Let's put this exact same requirement into "regular chess" terms:

White to play and find a move that's not check, but threatens mate-in-one.

Sound better? OK, but it's exactly the same requirement as a Double Whammy, but worded "legally." Before going any further, I highly suggest you try solving the puzzle.

Quite a few of my students thought they found an answer fairly quickly and suggested 1.♘a3 followed by 2.♗f3. Can you "see" why this is not the correct solution?

The answer is that 2.♗f3 is illegal! Once the knight moves, the bishop is pinned to the king. Think this is a coincidence? Jeff often puts such "reasonable" possible, but incorrect, solutions in his clever puzzles.

When I first did this problem, I tried 1.♖c3 followed by 2.♘b4, making use of the pin. That's more Jeff's type of solution, to create a pin. However, this obviously does not work as Black is not in mate since he has ...♔b7.

Need a hint? First, what are all the squares that White needs to attack that he is not attacking now that would accomplish the feat?

The answer is three: b7, c6, and d5. If you missed c6, as several have done, it's because you have to remember to attack the king too, or it's not mate!

Follow-up hint: there are two ways the solution might be accomplished: first, cover some of the three squares and then finish him off with a mate. For example, 1.♖xd7 to cover b7 and d5, then a check.

The second way is to cover all three squares at once, as 1.♘a3 and 2.♗f3 attempted to do. Which of the two do you think the answer will be?

If you guessed the second way, you are correct.

Now the final hint: which pieces, if placed on a different square than now, could attack all three squares?

The answer is that the light-squared bishop or the queen could go to f3, g2, or h1. Going to a8 doesn't work as ...♔b7 stops mate and e4 would not be mate due to ...fxe4.

But we tried ♘a3 and ♗f3 to cover b5 and free the bishop, so that doesn't work. Therefore, can the queen get to f3, g2, or h1 in two moves? Of course!

So the answer is **1.♕a1** followed by **2.♕h1 mate**.

Was that so difficult? Turns out it is. I once gave this puzzle to three players with an average rating of 2000 while we waited for the pairings at our Main Line Chess Club in Gladwyne, Pennsylvania.

In the ten minutes the three were looking, none of them was able to find it.

I believe this is one of the great board-vision puzzles I have seen. A queen in the upper right quadrant has to move to the lower left quadrant to go to the lower right quadrant to checkmate a king in the upper-left quadrant! You have to be able to see the entire board to see the solution. See my Chess.com article, "The Amazing Power of Board Vision" at https://www.chess.com/blog/danheisman/the-amazing-power-of-board-vision.

Another note on this puzzle: since the current pieces are set up on the ranks, you have to think "outside the box" of action to move to the dormant first rank. Putting your queen *en prise* on the first move to the queen on a2 is just icing on the cake. Easy, right? No *en passants*, under-promotions, castling, pins, or anything. Just two "long" queen moves.

If you don't think that this is a wonderful board-vision problem, and think that doing problems like these won't help your play, I suspect your rating is a little lower than you would like it to be.

Puzzle #6
Don't jump to conclusions – think outside the box

The main ways an instructor can get an instructive puzzle are:

- Compose it,
- Get it from a game, or
- "Borrow" it from another source.

There are also "public domain" puzzles such as elementary back-rank mates. If I claim another author copied my back-rank mate example for his publication, I would get laughed out of court (at least chess public-opinion court). Anyone has free access to these generic, basic examples.

The puzzle below was borrowed from GM Jonathan Rowson's book *Chess for Zebras*, specifically because he states that he uses it in teaching to prove a point. Since this is Puzzles with a Point, what better type of puzzle to use? Moreover, it is the dreaded "Helpmate," so if you are feeling like only "White to play and win" will help make you a better player (no pun intended), then stop right here.

For those unfamiliar with helpmates, Black plays first and cooperates to help mate in a specific number of moves. This is a Helpmate in 2, so the sequence of moves will be Black-White-Black-White, where White's second move must be checkmate.

Black to move: Helpmate in 2 moves
Black

White

If you spend a minute on this problem, then you probably will find what most do: why can't White set up the standard mating sequence 2.♘f6 and 3.♕g8 mate? (Note: White is going second, hence his first move is #2.)

If this is the pattern, all Black has to do is to play dumb and cooperate. But how is he to do this? If 1...h1♕+ or 1....h1♖+, those are both check, so White does not have time to set up 2.♘f6 and 3.♕g8 mate.

If Black plays 1...h1♗, then after 2.♘f6 Black is in *Zugzwang*, and must spoil White's plans with 2....♗xg2, whether he likes it or not.

Finally, if Black plays 1...h1♘ then after 2.♘f6 Black is again in *Zugzwang:* 2...♘g3 blocks the queen's path to g8, or 2...♘f2+ and again White has to get out of check and does not have time for a mate. I guess it's not a coincidence the king was placed on d1 (although d3 or e4 might also do for this purpose).

Conclusion: The "obvious" pattern 2.♘f6 and 3.♕g8 mate doesn't work!

Oops!

That makes things more difficult (as they should be in a good problem). Back to the drawing board.

Using the same technique, "working backward" as was done with 2.♘f6 and 3.♕g8 mate, what other mating pattern with these few pieces can be accomplished? The white king cannot participate in two moves, so that leaves the ensemble of the four other pieces. Does the black pawn participate in the mate pattern? If so, it would have to promote to a queen or rook because getting a knight or bishop would require more than two moves to help checkmate the black king (the piece would have to get close enough by the second move).

With these hints, several of my students eventually saw the point that Rowson was trying to make with his students. A little "outside the box" thinking is required once ♘f6 and ♕g8 mate is reluctantly rejected.

There is a mating pattern with a black rook blocking the king, but how to get there? **1...h1♖+!** So it's check after all. But how does White get the tempo he needs to reposition his queen? **2.♕f1.** Easy as pie! This is a helpmate. Black will kindly help by taking the "wrong" piece! **2...♖xh7 3.♕f8 mate.**

Not so hard once you see it. "Everything is easy if you know how." ☺

The "outside the box" solution was what Rowson was striving for. He wanted his students to be able to look at patterns that might be vaguely familiar and try to find moves and ideas that were not the same as the solutions they remember.

As I often tell my students, *"All that chess knowledge you get from studying patterns – openings, endgames, tactics – is extremely helpful, even necessary. But it does not replace the need to be good at analysis. Even if you see something similar to what you studied, you still have to analyze and say, 'That solution I remember from the studied pattern... does it really work here, or can I find a flaw in trying to apply it?'"*

Applying a known solution to an "only-similar" position blindly can often lead to trouble...

Puzzle #7
Where do your eyes go?

This Puzzle with a Point is another borrowed one, but I don't remember the source. However, as soon as I saw this puzzle, I thought, "I need this type of puzzle among the ones I give my students!" So here it is:

White to move
Black

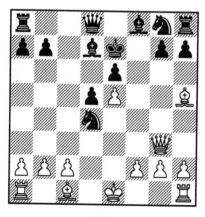

White

The first thing that jumps out to almost everyone is the enormous "Seed of Tactical Destruction" that the black king and queen are now on the same h4-d8 diagonal, suggesting a move like 1.♗g5+ when Black has little choice but to start tossing material. What could be easier?

So they start analyzing 1.♗g5+ and are quite pleased to find that Black is forced to play 1...♘f6, putting the knight in position to be captured by the pawn on e5, with check no less.

Occasionally a student even stops at this point and say, *"1.♗g5+ Final answer"* (I use "final answer" as in the game show "Who Wants to Be a Millionaire?" so that I know when my students are finished. This has the added benefit of simulating when they would hit the clock in a real game, and knowing when to stop thinking and make the move and hit the clock is an enormously underrated chess skill).

There's a problem with stopping at 1.♗g5+, though.

The students who stop there usually did not count the material.

> Count the material before doing a problem.
> It's very likely that there is no sense winning
> material if it still leaves you losing.

It turns out Black is ahead two pieces. To be technically correct, Black is ahead two knights for a pawn but, when you get multiple pieces ahead, the number of pawns in compensation would have to be large for it to be worth adding. That means if White plays 1.♗g5+ ♘f6 and wins the knight with say, 2.exf6+ gxf6, then, by material alone, White is not ahead a piece (as he would be if the position had started with even material), but still behind a piece.

Moral of the story: count the material before doing a problem. It's very likely that there is no sense winning material if it still leaves you losing.

White actually has a way to win two pieces with a "better" check, 1.♕h4+. Then after the forced 1...♘f6, 2.exf6+ gxf6 3.♕xd4 not only snags the other knight, but prevents ...♘xc2+ in the process.

When you see a good move, don't play it. Look for a better one.

Are we finished?

No, we have seen two moves but we should not stop looking for a better one. In fact, analyzing those two moves would not be the best way to start this (or most) problems. The best way would be to start by listing all the possible forcing moves (checks, captures, and threats) that should be investigated and *then* start analyzing one that is most likely to meet our goals. This is also consistent with the principle, *"Find the best plan and then find the move that best meets it."*

All of White's checks are: 1.♗g5+, 1.♕h4+, 1.♕g5+, 1.♕xg7+, and 1.♕a3+. Which is the most promising?

Look Wide Before You Look Deep.

Despite the Seeds of Tactical Destruction on the dark squares on the kingside, which should encourage your eyes to look there first, **1.♕a3** ...is **mate!** So that must be the answer and that means if you just had listed all the checks and found the most promising one, you would not have had to analyze any of the other moves. To do so would be a waste of time.

The final point of this puzzle is that you should follow Cecil Purdy's advice and *Look Wide Before You Look Deep*. Also, look around the entire board. Just because your eye is drawn to a certain area (as it most certainly should be in this clever setup), that doesn't mean there are not candidate – and even "best" – moves that can be played on or to the "other" portions of the board

Puzzle #8
Quiescence errors

This puzzle has a very clear point. Very weak players will likely get it wrong, and less weak players would also likely make the wrong move if it occurred in a game.

But that's one of the points of this puzzle: things are much easier in a puzzle when you know something is there, rather than in a game, where no one holds up a sign saying, *"Wait! Don't move! There's something here and don't move until you find it!"*

This, of course, is exactly what doing a puzzle does for you. This "Don't stop!" idea also helps explains what causes quiescence errors (see Chapter 11). A quiescence error is where you stop analyzing too early and miss checks, captures, and/or threats of consequence that would change your evaluation of the line.

In a game, without the "Don't Move!" sign, many lower-rated players simply stop every time they see that a move loses material, no matter how simple the problem would be if you told them, "Look a little further..."

Good players don't make this error, in puzzles or in games. Instead of saying, *"This move loses material; I won't play it,"* they ask:

"This move loses material; is there any further forcing move (check, capture, or threat) that would make it worth my while to continue investigating?"

If the answer is No, then they, too, stop analyzing. But if the answer is Yes, then they look further. A good general rule is: *if the possible reward is greater than the initial risk, it is worth continuing.* So you would not consider sacrificing a queen with the possible chance to win a rook, but you would consider sacrificing anything (i.e., not stop analyzing no matter how much material was sacrificed) if there were still the possibility of a forced mate in that line.

White to move
Black

White

In this puzzle, weak players might think, *"Oh, if I play 1.♕xd4, I lose my queen to 1...♗xd4, so I can't do that"* and play some other move (again, less likely in a puzzle than in a game!).

However, stronger players would undoubtedly instead think, *"Suppose I play 1.♕xd4 and he plays 1...♗xd4. Then after 2.♗xd4 I am threatening 3.♖h8 mate. Therefore, it is worth investigating further to see if Black can stop this by blocking the diagonal with something like ...f7-f6. If he can't, then 1.♕xd4 looks like it might be mating."*

Their investigation would continue after **1.♕xd4 ♗xd4 2.♗xd4.** Now Black would love to play 2...f6, but that is illegal due to the bishop on c4 which is pinning the f-pawn. That's not a coincidence, considering this is a puzzle!

So what can Black do? Putting the queen on the long diagonal only delays things, but Black actually has a way of moving the f8 rook with check, so we must investigate... **2...♕xe2+.**

However, now White can capture the queen and, at the very least, he will be ahead a piece, justifying 1.♕xd4. In fact, many players would stop analyzing here, double-check the lines, and play 1.♕xd4. But for fun, let's look a little further: **3.♔xe2.** Keeping the pin on the a2-g8 diagonal and preventing 3...f6. **3...♖fe8+.** Forced, so the black king can escape toward f8 and e7 **4.♔f1 ♔f8.** Throwing in 4... ♗xg2+ or 4...♖e1+ 5.♖xe1 does delay matters but qualifies as spite checking. Now how can White not just stay ahead a piece, but finish off the mate? **5.♗f6** and Black will be mated soon with ♖h8 mate.

The computer points out that Black can last longest with 1.♕xd4 ♕xe2+ but the problem could be labeled, *"White to play and mate in 9,"* since that's the longest Black can last.

Moral of the story: even in games, don't fall for the common quiescence error by rejecting moves like 1.♕xd4 out of hand. Check to see if they might be worth investigating. Remember, good players use almost all their time every game; sometimes these seemingly low-probability moves are the ones that turn out to win the game.

Puzzle #9
If you see a good move...

Our final puzzle is from a real game I watched online. A student was playing White in a 45 45 game and he had played too fast. In this deep endgame position he had over 50 minutes remaining on his clock, more than the amount with which he started the game!

White to move
Black

White

Not only has Black blundered with his previous move of ...♔f5 but, thankfully, my student actually took note and finally slowed down to consider his move. This seemed to indicate that he might realize he was not only back in the game, but in command.

So I waited for his move. A few minutes passed and, unfortunately, he played 1.♗b6? to guard the promotion square. Can you see what he missed?

1.♗d6! is the winner, trying not just to win a rook, but going for the queen!

Black can check, but if White zigzags his king toward the rook on the b- and c-files, the black rook can never safely reach the eighth rank, where b8 and c8 are covered by the bishop and pawn, respectively: **1...♖c1+ 2.♔b5 ♖b1+ 3.♔c4 ♖c1+ 4.♔b3 ♖b1+ 5.♔c2** and White wins.

Instead, after 1.♗b6? the game continued 1...h5 2.d8♕ ♖xd8 3.♗xd8 ♔g4 4.♔d5 ...and White managed to draw.

Moral of the story: promotion tactics are tricky things. Sometimes your pawn gets stopped, sometimes the opponent has to give up a piece to stop it, and sometimes, if he falls asleep and you are alert, you can get an entire queen. Again a case of, *"If you see a good move* (such as winning a rook), *look for a better one* (getting a queen) – *you are trying to find the best move you can in a reasonable amount of time.*

Chapter 15

//

Illustrative Games

A lthough the games in this chapter were played by very low-rated players and many of the errors are fairly elementary, these errors represent some of the common recurring problems discussed throughout this book. Moreover, these errors are not relegated to players of ratings this low; similar errors are often made by players with much higher ratings.

Game 1:
In this game, Black was a student of mine, about age 7, who had been taking lessons for a couple of months (my students have ranged in age from 5 to 75...). He knows about the center and developing his pieces. He knew the value of the pieces and my Number 1 guideline, *"Before you move, visualize your possible moves and make sure all your pieces would be safe; check to see if your opponent's pieces are safe; if not, consider taking them off."* He also knows the guideline, *"If you see a good move, look for a better one."* White is a friend of his, about 9 years old. The extra age difference will about make up for the difference in knowledge, as White has never had any lessons...

	White (400)	**Black** (500)
1.	g3	e5
2.	c4	♘f6
3.	a3	♘c6
4.	a4	

White wastes time moving a pawn twice. He does not know the guideline, *"Move every piece once before you move any piece twice, unless there is a tactic."* Note that you don't need to move every *pawn* once but, for the most part, you don't want to move a pawn twice unless it does something very positive, like forcing a stronger piece to move to a weaker square. In general, moving two pawns in the opening is not enough (usually your pieces get cramped for lack of space, which pawns provide), so moving four or five in the first 15 moves or so is reasonable.

> ## Move every piece once before you move any piece twice, unless there is a tactic.

4...	♗b4
5. ♖a2	d6

So far, Black is following normal development guidelines and White is not, so Black has already built up a huge advantage. However, at this level this type of advantage is relatively meaningless. The player who leaves the fewest pieces *en prise* and takes off the most of his opponent's will usually win.

6. g4?	♘xg4

When going over the game, I asked Black if he should take the g-pawn with the knight or the bishop. He correctly replied, *"The bishop"* and, when asked why, correctly said, *"Because the bishop has not moved yet."* This answer, along with the fact that he took with the knight instead, illustrates that even though beginners may know what is right, they often do not play it just because they don't take the time to think.

7. **f3??**

Black (500)

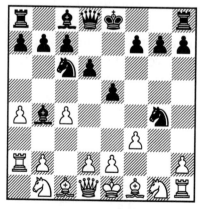

White (400)

7...   **♘f2???**

Black sees a fork of the rook and queen, but overlooks several basic factors, such as that 7...♕h4 instead is checkmate, and that after 7...♘f2, the knight can just be taken with 8.♔xf2. After the game I reminded Black to look for all checks, captures, and threats. I asked him how many checks he had. He said two. I asked him if either one was good. He replied, *"7...♕h4 is mate." "So why didn't you play it?" "I didn't look."*

8. ♕c2??

White also sees the fork and reasons that since his queen is attacked, he ought to move it. This is the exact same problem as someone who is checked and automatically touches his king to move out of check when he could just capture the checking piece for free. The logic, "X is attacked, so I must move X" is, of course, faulty. In chess there are often better ways of protecting X (especially in beginners' games!), such as removing the attacker.

8...   **♘xh1**
9. ♗h3??   **♗xh3**
10. ♔d1??

White does not recapture on h3 with the knight. At this point the scoresheet became undecipherable as to the exact moves, mainly because the scorekeeper was playing Black, and for beginners it is more difficult to record algebraic with Black. However, what happened was that Black was winning by a large margin until he left his queen in take to an opposing queen. His opponent, then up a queen and a piece for two rooks, was unable to figure out how to win and *agreed to a draw...*

Game 2:

	White (500)	**Black** (1000)
1.	e4	c5
2.	d3	d6

3. ♗f4

White forgets what I had suggested earlier in the day, "Knights usually are developed before bishops."

3...	♘c6
4. ♘f3	♘f6
5. d4?	

White moves a pawn twice before finishing the development of his pieces. He also forgets to check to see what the pawn was doing before, which was defending his e-pawn.

5...	cxd4
6.♘bd2	

Now he guards his e-pawn, but at the cost of having lost his d-pawn.

6...	g6
7. e5	dxe5
8. ♘xe5	♗g7
9. c4	dxc3 *e.p.*
10. bxc3	0-0

The contrast between what a 1000 player knows and what a 500 player knows is large. Black has calmly developed his pieces and castled; White has somewhat aimlessly moved a couple of pieces. But on the next move, White's game starts to fall apart badly.

11. g4?

This move is bad for several reasons: it does not develop a piece, it loses a pawn, and it weakens the king's position. When my son was young, he still sometimes made this mistake, forgetting to ask himself, *"If I make this move, where can my king go where it will be safe for the rest of the game?"*

11...	♘xe5

Congratulations to Black for recognizing this position as a "removal of the guard" tactic. He captures the knight which was defending the g-pawn, thus leaving the g-pawn exposed to capture next move.

12. ♗xe5　　　　　　♗xg4

Black (1000)

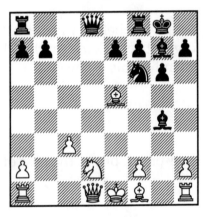

White (500)

13. ♗g2??

White doesn't see that his queen is attacked. This goes right under the lesson about the mistaken logic, "If his piece is doing one thing, it probably isn't doing another." White reasoned, *"The bishop went to g4 to take my pawn. So I know the purpose of that move. Now I can go ahead and look at what I should do."* Wrong! See Chapter 7, "Just Because It's Forced..."

13...　　　　　　♗xd1
14. ♖xd1　　　　　♕a5

(see diagram next page)

Black (1000)

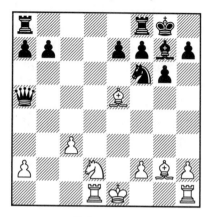

White (500)

15. ♗(e5!)xb7 (illegal move)

Black (1000)

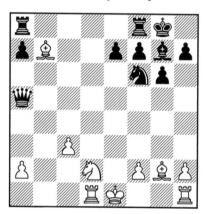

White (500)
Position after 15.♗(e5!)xb7 (illegal)

White has accidentally moved the wrong bishop! Now he makes a big mistake. I reminded him a few times that morning, *"If anything strange happens in your game, stop the clock and get the tournament director."* Moving the wrong bishop illegally certainly qualifies as strange!

Black now said, *"That is illegal. You moved the wrong bishop."* Black then replaces his pawn on b7 and the illegally moved white bishop is placed on the neighboring square, c7 – even though it originally came from e5! Black looked at the board, indicated the bishop now on c7, and asked, *"Is that your move?"* White, who was a teenager and not a youngster, was still flustered and quickly answered *"Yes"* even though he really had no reason to move the bishop to c7 where it is *en prise*. However, by touch move, he had to move the bishop on e5 somewhere.

Black (1000)

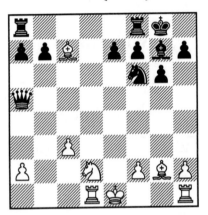

White (500)
Position after 15.♗c7 (legal move)

15...	♕xc7

And, soon thereafter, Black won easily. After the game, I asked White, *"Why did you let your bishop stay on c7 where Black could take it? After all, the touch-move rule required you to move that bishop, but since you took your hand off it on an illegal square (b7), you could replace it where you came from, e5, and move it anywhere you wanted."*

White replied something like, *"I didn't know."* I said, *"Then that is your fault, because I had said several times that if there is something strange going on where you don't know what the rule is, what should you do?"* "Stop the clock and call the tournament *director,"* he immediately replied. *"So you didn't, and you just lost a piece for nothing."*

This type of error is not uncommon among players of all ages playing in their first tournament or club game. They are so nervous that they allow all kinds of crazy things to happen in their game which would not occur if they were thinking normally or had the presence of mind to get the tournament director.

Game 3:

	White (900)	**Black** (500)
1.	e4	e5
2.	♘f3	♘c6
3.	♗b5	♗b4

Black, of course, does not know Ruy López opening theory, but disregards the guideline "knights before bishops." Instead he mimics his higher-rated opponent, but while White's bishop move prepares castling and puts pressure on the black knight and the e5 square, Black's counter has no real purpose.

4.	0-0	♘f6
5.	d3	d5??

Black makes several mistakes with this move. First, he fails to notice that by moving his d-pawn, he pins his queen's knight to his king (he should have asked himself, *"I am planning ...d5; what is the effect of this move on my other pieces?"*) and thus he is removing his own guard and losing his e-pawn. Black is also starting counter-action in the center when his opponent is castled and he is not – often a recipe for disaster.

6.	♘xe5	g5?

Black not only does not guard his knight on c6, which is attacked twice, but he puts another pawn in take and ruins his kingside pawn field. This is one time I cannot comment on what he must have been thinking; I couldn't figure it out – I thought 6...g5 was a misrecorded move, but Black said that was what he played. He also could not explain why he played 6...g5.

7.	exd5	0-0??

Black panics and continues to follow general principles unwisely. I always tell my students that piece safety (including king safety) takes precedence over all other chess considerations. So, in this instance, the fact that White is attacking the black knight with a pawn is far more important than Black's need to castle early. Of course, advanced players can come with counter-examples where this might not be true, but 99.9% of the time just giving up large amounts of material is not correct. It is important for beginners to comprehend that they should wait until they understand the game better before they start to apply the exceptions!

8.	dxc6	bxc6
9.	&c4	&e8?

Black (500)

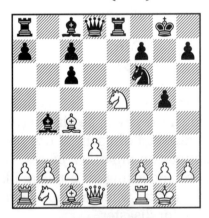

White (900)
Position after 9...&e8?

This is another example of, *"Just because it's forced it can't be doing something else."* White thought he had to move his bishop on move 9 (although he could just have captured the c-pawn) and

Black thought so, too. Thus Black did not stop to look and see that the bishop, which had just moved to avoid capture by the pawn, also positioned himself to attack the f7 square. Of course Black is still following the general principle of, *"Developing all your pieces toward the center"* and did not realize his f7 square is now inadequately defended. *Almost always, tactics (safety) takes precedence over these strategic and positional principles.*

> Almost always, tactics (safety) takes precedence over strategic and positional principles.

10. ♕e1???

White finally returns the favor and more. He also fails to see that Black's move is not much of a threat on the knight and that he can guard his knight by either capturing the pawn on f7 with 10.♘xf7 or capture the attacking rook with 10.♗xf7+ ♔-moves 11.♗xe8, either way with an enormous advantage. Instead he guards his knight by "developing" his queen. Of course, it would have been better to choose a defense which does not lose so much material!

10... ♗xe1
11. ♖xe1 ♖xe5??

Black makes yet another "Just because it's forced..." error. As the reader can probably tell by now, this kind of error is much more common among beginners than one might think. Black feels that since he has just captured the defender of the knight, he can now freely take the knight. Black knows that a rook is worth almost two pawns more than a knight, but he didn't take the time to see that the knight was now defended by White's recapture. Once my students eliminate this type of basic error of making quick assumptions and playing too fast, they usually get a lot better!

12. ♖xe5

At this point Black got tired of going over this game, and I can't say I blame him! Of course, *going over your games to learn about your mistakes, especially with a better player, is about the best thing you can do to improve your game.* No book or computer can look at what you did and tell you that you played too fast or too slow or that you misapplied the general principles, or give you other vital feedback that will help you learn.

We didn't finish analyzing the game, but **White,** who first was winning easily, then losing, and is now probably better (he has a rook, a bishop, and a pawn for the queen, along with the bishop pair) **won.** So even though Black won the queen for a bishop, it wasn't enough to overcome the large amount of skill and knowledge between a 900 player and a 500 player.

Game 4:

The following game fragment is not spectacular, but represents several common mistakes. White, a young tournament player, is practicing against a computer. Computers are handy practice opponents – they are always available, never get tired, and don't complain when they lose. Also, you can set the computer to any level you want. I suggest that, *whenever possible, you play an opponent about 50-200 USCF rating points above you.* This means you should win about 25-45% of the games. This is approximately the optimum level where your opponent is properly "pushing" you; any higher and you lose too much for it to be fun (and lose too badly for the game to be instructive); any lower and you are not being punished enough for your mistakes. This 50- to 200-point guideline of course applies whether you are setting a computer level or trying to figure out which section of a tournament would be most beneficial to play in. Note that playing some weaker opponents is also necessary to learn good technique and to give you the joy of winning occasionally!

The opposite argument – and a good one – is that *if you want to be good against humans, play humans.* Computers don't play like humans in many ways, and the mistakes they make to play at a weak level are often quite different from the mistakes a human opponent might make. Moreover, human opponents can review the game with you and will likely play at a humanly pace. So while computers are easily available opponents, if you have a choice, I would always go with practicing against a human.

	White (600)	**Black** (Computer set to "Easy")
1.	**e4**	♘c6
2.	♘f3	

White has been taught to get out his kingside pieces and castle early; but he has also been taught to set up the "little center" – d4 and e4 – whenever his opponent lets him. With 1...♘c6, his opponent has allowed the little center, but White ignores his opponent and plays as if 2.d4 has been prevented.

2...	♘b4

The computer, set on "Easy," violates the strong principle, *"Don't move any piece in the opening twice until you move all of your pieces once – unless there is a tactic* (the move wins material or mates or prevents from losing material/mate.)"

3.	♗c4	b5?

The computer gives a free pawn. It is hard to see how a decent human could lose to a computer playing like this, but unfortunately humans have the capacity to make a large blunder that can make up for all the computer's (intentional) little blunders.

4.	♗xb5	c6
5.	♗c4	d5

Black attacks both the bishop and the e-pawn. More experienced humans would see that the easiest solution is to first capture the pawn with 6.exd5 and then move the bishop after the e-pawn is no longer attacked. Instead, White simply sees that his bishop is attacked by a pawn and moves it...

6.	♗e2?	♗g4?

The computer does not capture the e-pawn, which of course is the best move. Now that his bishop is safe, White sees that he must save the e-pawn.

7. exd5 &xf3

Black voluntarily gives up the bishop pair, which is worth on average about half a pawn!

8. &xf3 cxd5
9. 0-0 &d6
10. d4 &xa2??

Black (Computer set to "Easy")

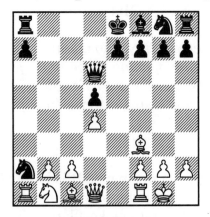

White (600)
Position after 10...&xa2??

The computer gives away a piece in the easiest manner – he moves it *right in front* of a piece that can take it for free...

11. &e3??

But the human does not make the capture! There are two possible explanations for this failure to take the free knight. Either White made a board-vision error and thought that the queen on d6 was guarding the knight (thus misreading the diagonal force of the queen) or he had already decided it was time to develop the bishop and was going to do so no matter what Black moved. In either case, this is an example of why beginning humans have so much trouble – they do not carefully look at their opponent's moves and, when given some great opportunities, do not take the time to consider how they might take advantage of them.

11... ♘b4

Black gets away scot-free.

12. ♘c3

White is doing a commendable job of developing all his pieces. Unfortunately, he has been missing the forest for the trees on a number of his moves.

12... a6
13. ♕d2 ♘f6
14. ♖ad1

White continues to blindly follow opening guidelines, such as bringing rooks to the center. Unfortunately, since he has lost his a-pawn already, the rook stood well on a1 and it was not beneficial to bring the rook to the center behind the fixed d-pawns! You might call this an example of *Rote* over *Right*.

14... e6
15. ♖fe1

White completes his development and, with the material even, it would look to a casual observer passing the game at this point that so far all has gone normally!

15... ♗e7
16. h3

As so often happens, a young player completing his development runs out of ideas. In this case, he solves his problem of what to do by creating *Luft* for his king.

16...	a5
17. ♖a1	

White now realizes (via Black's pawn move) that his rook is better served on the semi-open a-file.

17...	♛b6
18. ♔h2	

But now White again decides to temporize and actually moves his king to a more vulnerable square along the open b8-h2 diagonal.

At this point the human had to **abandon the game** (dinner time?). The position, after all the earlier ups and downs, is fairly even. Let's see the same two opponents in action again:

Game 5:

White (600)	**Black** (Computer set to "Easy")
1. e4	a6

On its easy level, Black gives White the center willingly.

2. d4

This time White does seize the "little center."

2...	d5
3. exd5	♛xd5
4. ♘c3	

This time White plays the first few moves perfectly, attacking the queen with gain of tempo. White has a comfortable advantage but, as we have seen, such a lead at this level is not necessarily likely to lead to victory!

4...	♛d7
5. ♘f3	

White correctly develops "knights before bishops."

5...	♕e6
6. ♗e2	b5

Black has a mild "threat" of ...b5-b4, driving the knight away from the center. White should see this by asking himself, *"What can Black do to me now that he couldn't do to me before?"* and get the answer 7...b4. However, there is nothing terribly wrong with White's next move.

7. 0-0	b4
8. ♘b1(?)	

White avoids 8.♘a4, knowing *"knight on the rim, your future is dim,"* except that b1 is also a rim square. Beginners tend to see the a-file and h-file as "more rim" than the first or eighth ranks, but for the most part these are all rim squares. Because of the awkward placing of Black's queen, better is 8.♘a4, when the knight may soon re-enter the game via c5.

8...	♗b7
9. ♗d3?	

White violates the strong principle, *"Don't move any piece in the opening twice until you move all of your pieces once – unless there is a tactic."* Except for not keeping their pieces safe, this is the most commonly violated opening principle by beginners.

9...	♕c6

Black lines up his queen and bishop to aim at the g2 square on the kingside. If White doesn't pay attention to this obvious "battery," and later moves the knight, he may find himself mated no matter how much he was winning.

10. ♗f4	♘d7
11. ♘bd2	

White correctly gets all his pieces developed towards the middle and retains his slight advantage.

| 11... | ♛f6 |
| 12. g3(?) | |

White sees that his bishop on f4 is attacked, and so guards it. But *there are five ways to make sure that a piece which is attacked is not lost: 1) move it, 2) guard it, 3) put something in the way, 4) counterattack, or 5) capture the threatening piece.* Beginners often do not consider all the alternatives. Here 12.g3 is the wrong way to guard the bishop because it weakens the light squares on the kingside, especially with the black bishop on b7 bearing down on the long diagonal.

12...	0-0-0
13. ♛e2	♚b8
14. ♖ad1	

Just as in the previous game, White dutifully activates his rook by bringing it to the center. Instead, the rook could have been activated closer to Black's king by playing 14.a3, threatening to capture the black b-pawn and to open up the a-file for the rook.

| 14... | ♚c8 |
| 15. ♖fe1 | ♚b8 |

The "Easy" computer does not see anything constructive, and so just moves its king back and forth.

| 16. ♘c4 | |

White is making progress, as his centralized pieces give him the advantage.

| 16... | ♚a7 |
| 17. ♘h4? | |

White now must move some pieces twice, but doesn't know what to do. He actually makes a move that is worse than Black's "nothing" moves of shuffling the king to and fro. Back to *"knight on the rim..."*

17...   **♛c6**

Black is programmed to threaten mate in ones. White sees the mate on g2, but he apparently sees neither that his knight on h4 is guarding g2 nor *all* the things that 17...♛c6 does. Therefore, he plays...

18. ♛f1???

Black (Computer set to "Easy")

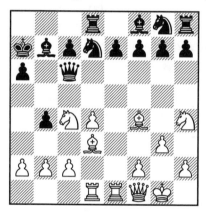

White (600)
Position after 18.♛f1???

...instead of properly blocking the diagonal by playing something like 18.♝e4, and thus does not stop the "other" mate, the one he missed:

18...   **♛h1 mate**

Once again we see the same pattern as in the previous computer game: the human follows several small general principles to get an advantage, but eventually makes an enormous tactical error to throw it all away on one move.

Chapter 15

It only takes one bad move to lose the game!

That is why, in chess, *intermediate* players can play well for 5, 10, or 20 moves in a row, but then let down their guard with one bad move and often lose, while good players know that if they let up their concentration on *any* move, it will likely negate all that effort they put in for all the previous moves of the game. Therefore, good players try to play their best on every move – no exceptions. Notice also that Black never moved any of his kingside pieces, yet won anyway due to White's tactical error.

Conclusion: Almost all beginning players make similar errors. The best cure is to play as often as you can, take your time, be careful to keep your pieces safe, and learn as much as you can about all the wonderful things a chessplayer needs to know to play better and even more enjoyable games. I hope this book has taken you one large step along the way to doing so!